"This is a great book for parents looking to strengthen their children's Christian faith."

—Dr. Stephen L. Cook
Professor of Old Testament,
Virginia Theological Seminary

"Growing the souls of the next generation is not a process which we can leave to the internet, television, and other media, assuming that religious affiliation is enough and neglect spiritual education. Bob Flanagan's work provides tools that must be part of contemporary society's new awareness of and efforts to curtail our nation's measured loss of its soul."

—Rev. Paul S. Briggs
Antioch Baptist Church,
Bedford Hills, New York

"As a parenting how-to, *Growing a Soul* is overflowing with insight and practical guidance from a passionate pastor of youth and a caring parent of teenagers. Parents will find it a terrific resource for many years."

—Harold G. Koenig, M.D.
Professor of Psychiatry & Behavior Sciences
Duke University Medical Center

Growing a Soul

Growing a Soul

A PRACTICAL GUIDE *to* RAISING YOUR
CHILD *with* SPIRITUAL INTELLIGENCE

BOB FLANAGAN

Pleasant Word
A Division of WINEPRESS PUBLISHING

Pleasant Word (a division of WinePress Publishing, PO Box 428, Enumclaw, WA 98022) functions only as book publisher. As such, the ultimate design, content, editorial accuracy, and views expressed or implied in this work are those of the author.

ISBN 13: 978-1-4141-1086-8
ISBN 10: 1-4141-1086-3
Library of Congress Catalog Card Number: 2007906577

To my mom and first spiritual mentor,
Winifred Grace Flanagan

Contents

Acknowledgments

I wrote this book because ten years ago, when my children were four and six, my wife and I couldn't find a resource to help us develop our children's faith and teach them why faith was important. We wanted to teach them how and why to pray. We wanted to teach our children why it is so good to make faith, especially faith in *God* through Jesus Christ, the center point of their lives. So I wrote this book with the decades-old memories of my family in my mind. And it is because of the encouragement of my wonderful wife and faith partner, and my two gifts from God, that this book has come into fruition.

Proverbs 15:22 says that success is found in the counsel of many. When it comes to this work, I must acknowledge the help, advice, insight, and counsel of many. My dear friends Jeanne Walker Bourland, Andrew Cregan, and C.J. De Santis and their families were very helpful and encouraging. They and their families were the first to use the forty devotions found in the second half of this book. I am indebted to them for their eagerness to use these devotions with their families. I must also acknowledge the invaluable help and advice of the small group of parishioners at St. Matthew's Church, Bedford, New York, who participated in the parenting and faith class that led to the first five chapters of this book. I am very appreciative to Leslie and Ross Henshaw, Kelley and Scott Johnston, Denise and Camillo Santomero, and Michelle and Doug Schimmel. Their advice and criticisms were invaluable in shaping the revisions of the opening chapters. Additionally, I thank the Rev. Dr. Paul Briggs and Martha Barnett for their careful and thoughtful reading and criticism.

There are two very special people I need to thank. My mentor, motivator, mirror, and model in ministry, the Reverend Terence L. Elsberry, has shown me how to be a pastor, priest, and leader. Without Terry's encouragement, patience, friendship, and openness to the Holy Spirit, I would not have been able to create this work. I know no one who preaches better, prays better, or is more open to being led by the Spirit than Terry Elsberry. I am humbled and blessed to serve as his colleague. I must also thank Jennifer Burke. She has been my patient and faithful writing editor for more than seven years. Even though I was an English major with an emphasis in poetry writing at Trinity College, Hartford, Connecticut, Jennifer taught me how to write. As someone who has degrees in writing and theology and is a mother of several young children and a baby, she helped me shape my words into a cohesive work. Without her encouragement, I would not have sought to publish this work.

And I thank God through Jesus Christ. In my difficult early days of ministry, I prayed to God for help and guidance. One day, I sat quietly in one of the pews in the back of the resplendent white sanctuary of St. Matthew's Church. There, with soft beams of afternoon light pouring through the large, clear windows, God answered my prayer. He said to me, "Write." And three projects came to mind, this book being the second. During the years since I received this guidance from God, I have been able to grow as a priest, gaining invaluable experience and serving the fabulous

Acknowledgments

congregation at St. Matthew's. With my writing assignments in hand, I gained patience to remain at St. Matthew's and in turn have been able to mature into my priestly vocation.

Introduction

For more than a hundred years, into this century, IQ or "intelligence quotient" has held sway as the dominant measure of human developmental achievement and the quintessential human standard of prowess. Many feel that it is the predictor of life success. Yet IQ and its tests have had their controversies. Are we born with an innate IQ proficiency? Can our environment, our socioeconomic situation, or upbringing make a difference in our IQ score? Simply, is it fair? These questions have haunted IQ theory for many years.

The study of intelligence has been of interest since ancient times. However, it wasn't until the late nineteenth century, with the rise of intelligence testing, that the controversy began to crop up. With the rise of Darwin's theory of evolution by natural selection, a dark, controversial side of intelligence testing emerged. By the second decade of the twentieth century, studies were recommending that those with extremely low IQ scores be sterilized. Intelligence scores weren't the only factor, but the tests added merit to other more nonscientific determinations.

Prevalence of IQ test usage increased with World War I. Over one million men were tested[1], and because of the sheer volume of tests, the results were not used during the war for personnel placement. These tests, however, yielded much data. The data, as it was analyzed and the results published, fueled the intelligence controversy that asserted IQ was simply a matter of nature or genetics. This view had deep implications for race relations and the assimilation of immigrants. Some used the test results to promote segregation and discrimination. Some argued that different races were superior to others.

Standing in opposition to the nature or genetic view, others argued for a nurture or pro-environment view. But those who argued that environmental factors played significant roles in determining IQ test results were to wage an uphill battle against the nature viewpoint for many years. A 1946 study, which showed how intense social and academic intervention dramatically increased test scores, was quietly received. Still, the nurture or pro-environment viewpoint gained more acceptance. By the mid-fifties, wider acceptance for such intervention yielded programs like Head Start. The general conclusion about programs like Head Start was that IQ indeed could be increased.

By the second half of the twentieth century, the view on intelligence theory was changing. In 1983, Harold Gardener, a professor at Harvard UNIversity, wrote about his theory of multiple intelligences. He described seven intelligences. His multiple intelligences theory called into question the standard IQ testing[2]. Many teachers agreed with Gardener's viewpoint and have since adopted his theory, developing their curriculum to reflect these different learning modes and helping their students to learn.

Still, the controversy of IQ continued, even to the end of the twentieth century. Published in 1994, *The Bell Curve* by Richard Herrnstein and Charles Murray argued that intelligence is hereditary. This reignited the controversy all over again. Yet, the conclusions of IQ theory are best described in a *New York Times* article from the summer of 2006 where Sir Michael Rutter of the University of London said, "It doesn't really matter whether the heritability of IQ is this particular figure or that one. Changing the environment can still make an enormous difference."[3] And it is that conclusion that is most helpful, because in the mid-nineties IQ was about to get a big shove from another part of the human character.

In 1995, Daniel Goleman encapsulated the building research regarding a new standard of intelligence. A journalist by trade, he discovered the work of John Mayer, now at the University of New Hampshire, and Peter Salovey from Yale University, which highlighted the importance of emotional intelligence, or EI. Goleman revolutionized intelligence thinking with *Emotional Intelligence: Why It Can Matter More Than IQ.* Ten years later, EI is accepted as one of the most important aspects that separates leaders from followers. An offshoot, SEL, or Social Emotional Learning, has been used in school districts nationwide to improve children's behavior in school and at home.

More recently, wider, popular acceptance has been building for four separate, dynamic measures of intelligence: mental intelligence (IQ), emotional intelligence (EQ), physical intelligence (PQ), and spiritual intelligence (SQ). Stephen Covey in his book, *The Eighth Habit: From Effectiveness to Greatness*, develops SQ theory. Echoing Covey, Doug Lennick and Fred Kiel write in *Moral Intelligence: Enhancing Business Performance and Leadership Success* about how "our mental capacity to determine how universal principles–like those embodied by the 'golden rule'–should be applied to our personal values, goals and actions."[4] The interest in these four separate, dynamic measures has found its home not in the pop-psychology shelves of the bookstores but in the business section. Why? Because business leaders are interested in workers who are not just mentally capable, but also those who can get along with others and find satisfaction in their work.

In support of SQ is the work of Dr. Jim Loehr, a performance psychologist, and author Tony Schwartz. Loehr and Schwartz are senior partners at LGE Performance Systems. Their work with professional athletes, SWAT teams, FBI hostage rescue team members, critical care physicians and nurses, high school students, and even clergy has led them to develop the "four energies theory."[5] These parallel the popular concept of the four intelligences, which are physical, emotional, mental, and spiritual. Loehr and Schwartz detail their work in *The Power of Full Engagement: Managing Energy, Not Time, Is the Key to High Performance and Personal Renewal*. Their book describes the importance of managing the four energies. They argue that time is not as important as energy and how we manage our four energy sources determines how successful, rewarding, and productive we are in our lives.

Building on this base of knowledge and especially highlighting the work of Loehr and Schwartz, *Growing a Soul* explores the value of SQ, or spiritual energy. Chapter One looks at SQ's importance with relationship to the three other energies. Then, from a Christian perspective, the following chapters will explain how parents can develop and deepen their child's "spiritual energy well" and their SQ. Chapter Two looks at how you can become a saint for your child. By joining proven parenting modes with foundational Christian teachings, parents can learn how to nurture their child's SQ. Next, Chapter Three shows how passages from the New Testament, specifically the Sermon on the Mount, provide helpful parenting tools that help children dig deep spiritual wells. Chapter Four illustrates and discusses ways in which habits and rituals are keys to SQ development. Then in Chapter Five, I walk through Communion to show how parents can help children understand the importance of this central act of the Christian faith. Children who build their understanding of the Communion will have a key SQ tool and learn how to fill their wells with life-giving water. The final main chapter explores the benefits of SQ by looking at recent studies of teenagers, their religious habits, and the positive effect religion has on the life of teens.

The second part of the book provides parents with a set of devotions (a Bible reading, commentary, and questions) that a family can use to address specific issues. The devotions can also be used as a complete series for a family to use during a specific period, such as the season of Lent.

This work is designed to be a hands-on tool. It's a resource to which you can refer over and over again. You will gain the nuts and bolts skills that will build your spiritual confidence. It may have been years since you have read the Bible or prayed. If that is the case, then this book is for you. Even if you have been a faithful attendee at church, this book will help you teach your children and bring them up in and with faith. It's my sincere hope that through this work you will develop your child's "spiritual energy well" and SQ—and thereby deepen your own.

Part One

CHAPTER 1 ❧

The Four Energy Sources and Child Development

We race through our lives without pausing to consider who we really want to be or where we really want to go.
(Jim Loehr and Tony Schwartz,
The Power of Full Engagement)[6]

On any given Saturday or Sunday afternoon, the park behind my home echoes with the sounds of children, coaches, and parents participating in or watching a game. Children yell, "Pass!" Coaches shout instructions, and parents often scream out encouraging words to their children. A young person scores a goal or a run and the park erupts in a cacophony of delight. Later, chants of appreciation for a game well played rise up at the game's conclusion. Sometimes these games start very early in the morning and other times practices last until the last drop of sunlight has been wrung from the sky. I admire this dedication parents and other adults have to the developing physical lives of young people.

Parents' dedication to their children's physical development is very important. Jim Loehr and Tony Schwartz, in *The Power of Full Engagement*, identify physical energy as the foundational energy of the four energies critical to living a fulfilled life. They contend that everything we do requires energy, which comes from four sources: physical, emotional, mental, and spiritual.[7] As parents, our job is to ensure that all four energy sources fully develop in our children.

After physical energy (PQ) is emotional energy (EQ). Emotional energy usually develops naturally. As most children age, they grow in emotional maturity. They learn how to act by modeling the actions of parents, siblings, and friends. They test their learning through social interaction on the playing fields, in classrooms, and during other social events. In a healthy home environment, most children gain a support system that allows them to function in the world and recharge their emotional batteries at home. Going into the stressful world and coming home to recover from life's stresses creates a pattern that Loehr and Schwartz find optimal for energy development. Like lifting a heavy shovel of dirt out of a deep well, followed by rest before digging out another, our emotional energy develops slowly. Day by day, emotional energy grows as our children stretch and rest themselves.

Building on PQ and EQ energies is mental energy (IQ), the primary "stuff" of children's schooling. Math, reading, science, art, and music develop the intellectual wells of both the left and right brains. With each quiz, test, and exam, children's wells of mental energy deepen. As they learn more, they have more mental energy. The pattern of learning and rest typified in the annual school calendar provides opportunities for students to draw deeply from their wells and then refill them again. And as with all energies, mental growth happens best in this regular pattern of school and vacation.

Spiritual energy (SQ) builds on a solid foundation of PQ, EQ, and IQ. Loehr and Schwartz define spiritual energy broadly as a "connection to a deeply held set of values and to a purpose beyond our self-interest."[8] It's the answer to that most important question, "What is the purpose and meaning of my life?" They add that it is the "most powerful source of motivation, perseverance, and direction"[9] that we have in our lives. Like emotional energy, SQ develops in part through modeling. Children see their parents praying and they learn how to pray. Or when they read Bible stories with their parents, children learn the values taught in the Bible. By struggling with questions of meaning and purpose, children and adults develop their spiritual energy. With a deeply held set of values, children are better able to make critical decisions. When fully developed, spiritual energy pulses throughout "all dimensions of our lives."[10]

PQ, EQ, IQ, and SQ all work in tandem with each other. They work together in order to provide us with the ability to function at our best. For us to be our best, no one energy source can dominate the other areas. If that occurs, people are at risk to themselves and others. When all four areas are fully developed, people fully realize their potential. They become their fullest selves. The following story about a boat builder will be helpful for understanding how the four energies work together and how essential each is for children to live full and complete lives.

THE BOAT BUILDER

This morning is special. Jim, a boat builder, has arrived at the shipyard early while it is still quiet. Entering his workshop, he flicks on the lights. His latest creation glows a resplendent white. A smile crosses his face as he sips his coffee and admires his work. Today is the day his latest sailboat will be christened and then slid down the ramp, crashing into the water. Today it will leave his yard and begin to sail the ocean.

Jim walks closer to the boat. He looks over the hull. Rubbing his fingertips along the smooth, lacquered hull, again he smiles.

It is cool and sleek. Not one bump. He thinks, *You'll be fast.* One last time, he checks for gaps along the edges. He looks for fine cracks and finds none. He stands at the bow and closes one eye. He studies the curve extending down each side. He admires the graceful contour. Moving toward the stern, he steps up a ladder. But before he steps onto the deck, he leans over to admire its camber. Everything looks good. Still, he knows a smooth hull and solid decking are not enough for a boat to manage the swells and storms waiting for it on the seas. *Yes indeed, you'll be fast.* He sips his coffee. But your physical capability and beauty are not enough.

He looks astern. Grabbing hold of the wheel, he checks the motion of the rudder. Without a solid rudder, this boat will flounder. It will keep this boat away from the rocks and shoals. It will steer her through the waves. It will guide her to faraway ports. He thinks about the keel underneath his feet. Yes, and without the keel, she will be directionless. The wind and waves will be merciless. They will constantly push and pull this boat. They will attempt to exert their influence. Yes, without the keel and rudder, this boat can never leave the harbor.

He glances down at the compass in its housing and the adjacent GPS console, the Loran and sonar. Direction, he thinks. Whoever steers her will always need to know where they are and where they are heading. No one wants to be out of sight of land without a compass, and now with global positioning, whoever sails her will be able to point to the chart and see exactly where he or she is. He thinks of the chartroom below deck. He had ordered charts for the local bays and coast, and the entire ocean as well. These sailors will always have a destination and will know how to get there, he concludes.

Finally, he glances up at the mast. It is tall and sturdy. When he was an apprentice builder, he always thought the mast was the most important feature of the boat. "It's what makes the boat fast and exciting," he used to say. But now he sees it as both exciting and dangerous. When used correctly, the sail captures the wind's energy, powering the boat to its destination. A sail full of wind, racing across the sea, is thrilling, he thinks. But the sail can also power the boat into the rocks. Power without the wisdom to direct it correctly will only destroy the boat.

As Jim steps off the boat, he concludes that all parts of his beautiful creation are important and essential. The boat's hull, its body, gives it form and physical capability. The rudder and keel direct the boat through the water. The compass and charts give it direction. And the sail captures the wind's energy, driving the boat forward toward its goal or destination.

SELF-STUDY QUESTIONS

Name the boat's essential parts.
Given the four energy sources–physical, emotional, mental, and spiritual–identified by Loehr and Schwartz, correlate each part of the boat to the four energy sources.
In your view, is one of the energies more important than another?
How would you prioritize them?

THE FOUR ENERGY SOURCES: A CLOSER LOOK

The four energies have also been called intelligences. Thus, mental energy or capacity is also known as IQ. Emotional energy or capacity is known as emotional intelligence or EQ. Physical energy has been defined as PQ or physical quotient. I will use spiritual energy, spiritual intelligence, or SQ interchangeably. Loehr and Schwartz, being athletes and coaches, are accustomed to developing energy and capacities in athletes. Conversely, Daniel Goleman, Dr. Stephen Covey, and others use intelligences or quotients to define the very same thing. So as far as my discussion of a child's spiritual development, energy or intelligence are one and the same.

The development of the four energy sources follows normative child developmental patterns. Children first develop their physical capabilities, then their emotional and social capabilities, then cognitive and mental, and finally moral and spiritual. There is overlap within these areas as development occurs, but chiefly, we see that physical development, such as learning to walk, comes before a toddler's ability to happily separate from a parent. And any kindergarten teacher will tell you that a child must develop physical stamina and emotional stability in order to be able to learn to read and write. Equally, all three are needed for a child to develop the ability to make decisions about right and wrong and to understand the abstract concepts of spirituality.

Thus if we were to build a pyramid using the four energies, it would look like this:[11]

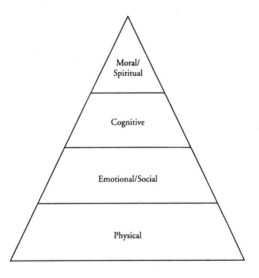

Physical energy (PQ) is the foundational source of energy. All energy is built upon our strength, stamina, flexibility, and resilience.[12] Physical energy allows us to live. It seems obvious, but when we are overworked, overweight, or overtired, our emotions are frayed, our thinking is sluggish, and we struggle to make good decisions.

Emotional and mental energies are the keys to modern life. They are measured just like physical energy. Strength, stamina, flexibility, and resilience play their parts in determining the depth of our emotional and mental wells. A deep emotional well gives us resilience in the face of disappointments and frustrations. A deep mental well helps us focus and concentrate on tasks and better solve problems.

While physical energy supports all of our other energies, without moral and spiritual energy children never will develop a sense of right and wrong, or, most importantly, a sense of purpose. So while physical energy is a child's foundation, spiritual energy gives guidance, purpose, and meaning. It is the capstone for all the other energies. For example, without a sense of right and wrong, physical strength leads to violence and abuse. Without a sense of something greater than self, a child's emotions turn inward toward selfishness, greed, and avarice. Without a sense of purpose, knowledge becomes trivia instead of wisdom.

The interaction between the energies looks like this:[13]

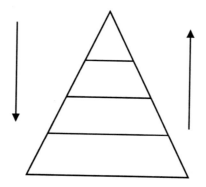

SELF-STUDY REFLECTION

Consider the importance of spiritual energy. Name three ways you can develop the spiritual energy capacity and capability in your child.

In the coming pages I will examine, from a Christian perspective, how parents can develop their children's spiritual energy or intelligence. I hope you will come to realize that spiritual development is as important as physical, emotional, and mental development. That coaching your daughter's soccer team is as important as being her Sunday school teacher. That reading the Bible with your son is as vital as helping him with his math homework. And that praying with your children at bedtime is essential to their long-term happiness, knowing who—and whose—they are, and where they want to go.

CHAPTER 2 ❧

The Parent's Four M's of Spiritual Guidance: How to Become a Saint for Your Child

Recite (the Lord's Commandments) to your children, and talk about them when you are at home and when you are away, when you lie down and when you rise.

(Deut. 6:7 NRSV)

I once heard Professor James Wallace describe how he interpreted the saints' lives and how they can influence our lives, which he details in his book *Preaching to the Hungers of the Heart.* He called it the four M's: mirror, mentor, model, and metaphor.[14] When looking at a parent's role as a former, developer, and nurturer of a child's faith, three of these M's fit: mirror, mentor, and model. The fourth, metaphor, I replace with motivator. Each of these four parenting modes provides opportunity to build your child's faith. These modes help us become saints for our children.

So what makes someone a saint? *The Oxford Dictionary of the Christian Church* notes the following: Saints were considered those who died because of their belief and faith in Jesus Christ. They were people who were close to God because of their holiness. And in some Christian denominations, saints were and are people who helped answer intercessory prayers. Historically, devotion and popularity of saints greatly expanded in the fourth century. During that period, the number of saints increased to include not just those who died for belief and faith in Jesus Christ, but also those who lived particularly devout and holy lives.[15]

During the Reformation, some denominations moved away from the focus on saints' aiding in intercessory prayer. In turn, wider definitions arose of who saints are and who can become a saint. In Lesbia Scott's hymn "I Sing a Song of the Saints of God," he defines saints as "patient and brave and true."[16] The hymn then continues to give examples of people who can be saints, such as: "And one was a doctor...and one was a soldier."[17] And then the hymn boldly claims, "there's not any reason, no, not the least, why I shouldn't be one too."[18] More recently, Donnie McClurkin, a noted gospel singer and pastor, sang "We Fall Down." The lyrics define a saint as "just a sinner who fell down and got up."[19] Over time, the definition of "saint" has varied, especially from denomination to denomination, but what is constant is that a saint is a faithful person whom we can admire and aspire to become more like.

Here's how the four modes parents can adopt to become saints for their children work. As a mirror, a parent reflects back to the child, the child's actions and/or emotions. For example, when one sibling is mean to another, as in taking away a toy, one way to help your child is to respond as a mirror. So Dad could say with empathy, "You know, in our family we share with each other. I know that it's hard to do it all the time, but try to think about how you would feel if she took your toy." That way Dad is mirroring to his daughter the feelings she caused in her sibling. Even more importantly, he is reflecting his calm, empathetic emotions about the situation. Mirroring is an effective teaching tool because it reflects the feelings of the hurt child toward the

other. It provides children with a means to see their actions
and how they affect others. Over time, children learn how to
empathize with other people.

Mirroring takes time for a child to understand, especially a
younger child. In *The Science of Parenting: How Today's Brain
Research Can Help You Raise Happy, Emotionally Balanced
Children*, Margot Sunderland writes, "The capacity to feel and
think deeply about another person's emotional pain or stress
levels develops slowly over time. Only after many hours of
showing your concern for them can you expect your children
to feel empathy."[20] So each time you underreact and stay
emotionally calm and even, you mirror empathy to your child
through your actions and words. Over time—years maybe—as
their higher brain functions develop, your child's ability to be
empathetic increases as well. Because of the length of time it
takes to develop empathy, mirroring may be the most difficult
of the four modes to develop, but the importance of empathy in
developing tolerance for others is worth the work. As your child's
saint, your ability to mirror back to your child, with patience
and kindness, helps him or her become more self-reflective and
understanding of others.

The role of the mentor is to provide guidance, often through
nurturing. My professor talked about saints as mentors in the
context of community. And that's right. As parents we often
mentor our children about social situations. Seemingly most
common is the situation of a child receiving something from
someone else. How many, if not all of us, have said, "Now, what
do you say?" This ubiquitous example of mentoring teaches our
children how to respond in a social setting. It's just being polite.
But, it's a very important lesson. Such simple lessons make up
the foundation of our society. Basic lessons such as this one
demonstrate the importance of parent mentors.

Moreover, mentoring helps children see how our teachings
apply in the real world. Dorothy Law Nolte and Rachel Harris

write in *Children Learn What They Live: Parenting to Inspire Values*, "Children learn what honesty is from their parents. What we do and what we say provide a living example of what it means to be honest."[21] Nolte and Harris go on to tell a story about a father and daughter leaving a restaurant. In the parking lot, the father realizes he received too much change from the cashier. They go back to the restaurant to return the extra money. Not only was the restaurant's staff surprised at and appreciative of the man's honest act, the father and daughter learned that the cashier would have had to make up the money himself. Imagine the message this father sent to his daughter for a few cents![22] Whether it is directing our children to be polite or showing our children honesty and integrity, mentoring helps our children see how positive values have positive effects. And in our actions, in doing the right things, we act like saints, too.

As models, parents show children how to act. Children watch how we act or react in situations and then try it out for themselves. We all have heard a young child blurt out a curse word—to the horror and shock of his or her parent. Quickly, the parent chides the child, "We don't use those words." But we also know, too, that the parent is kicking himself or herself for having used the word in the presence of the child.

Modeling is the one M over which we have the least control. As Nolte and Harris write, "Children are like sponges. They soak up everything we do, everything we say."[23] Unlike the other three, modeling happens whether we are conscious of it or not. Children of all ages—infant through teenager—watch our actions carefully. They watch us doing both good and bad. Thus, we are models to our children twenty-four hours a day and 365 days a year. Sometimes our children adopt our behaviors and other times they do the opposite. Either way, parental modeling remains a powerful influence.

Yet, in being models, parents are not expected to be perfect. In fact, it is important for children to see us make mistakes. "Children need to learn that it's all right to goof,"[24] writes William Sears and Martha Sears in *The Discipline Book: Everything You Need to Know to Have a Better-Behaved Child.* "You can lighten up the uptight child by modeling ways to handle mistakes,"[25] they add. While we tend to think of saints as perfect people, they weren't. Saints were special human beings, but they were still human and as such they made mistakes. As saints for our children, it is important for our children to see that we are human and make mistakes just like them.

The fourth M is motivator. At first blush, this mode seems to be the old "carrot or stick" method. For example, you can motivate a child to keep his or her room clean by rewarding an allowance, a classic carrot. Equally, if he or she constantly litters the room with dirty clothing, you can ground him or her until the room is clean, or even scoop up all the dirty clothes and make him or her buy them back–examples of stick. William and Martha Sears write, "Children and adults behave according to the pleasure principle: Behavior that's rewarding continues, behavior that's unrewarding ceases."[26] The motivator mode goes beyond reward or penalty. The goal, as noted by the Searses, is to help our children gain "self discipline."[27]

Our ability to control our emotional selves is a deep part of the religious life that has been passed on to us by saints. Drawing on Lesbia Scott's hymn, saints are "patient, brave and true." Consider how you can motivate your children by your own life if you embody those saintly traits. Equally, by motivating your children to be patient, they will be able to endure difficulties. If they are motivated to be brave, they will be strong in adversities. If they are motivated to be true to God, they always will have meaning and purpose to their lives, and a strong moral foundation. In motivating your children toward good behavior and worthy values, you help them gain self-discipline and in turn help them become saints, too.

Saints call us to higher ground, to strive for higher values and greater self-discipline. Saints mirror our faults to us by showing us who we are—"sinners who have fallen." Saints are mentors to us in that they show us how we can get back up. Saints model for us the way to live once we are back on our feet. And as motivators, saints call us to stay on our feet through self-discipline.

For further illustration of the four M's, consider the following story.

SAND CASTLES

For many summers, my son and I padded down the steps from Nanny and Poppy's lake house to the small sandy beach on the lake. There, we spent hours building sandcastles. With each passing summer not only did the shape, complexity, and artistry of our creations change, but also our roles as builders.

In the beginning, when he was only one-and-a-half, Dan plopped down on the sand with his bright, multicolored, floppy hat stuck on his head and his chubby body slathered in sunscreen. In one hand he clutched the handle of a yellow plastic bucket that was seemingly half his size. In his other hand was a little shovel. I splashed into the water and scooped up a pile of sand in a bucket, carried it back to the beach, and then flipped it over onto the sand in front of him. Tossing the bucket aside, I molded and shaped the sand into a simple castle. Dan babbled at me, encouraging me to build more.

The following summer our work together became more sophisticated. Dan donned a new bathing suit and with his thinned body making him more mobile, we worked side by side. I still lugged most of the wet moldable sand onto the beach from the water, but our work was different now.

The Parent's Four M's of Spiritual Guidance: How to Become a Saint for Your Child

He watched me build my castle and then he built one, too. I still gave him a pile of sand with which to work, but he shaped it with his shovel and carved it with his hands. If I built a moat, he dug one. If I added a tunnel, he dug one, too. If my castle had walls, so did his.

The following summer, he worked more independently. For hours he cruised back and forth from the water to the sand. He studied his creation, sometimes knocking it down or radically changing it. He would ask me for my opinion: "Daddy, come and look." I examined his progress. At times, I pointed out deficiencies in his work: "What do you think will happen if a big wave comes in? Will your walls withstand the wash?" Other times I gave him advice: "See the thickness of your walls? If you add more sand here, they will be stronger. Then you can make your castle taller."

As the summers went by, Dan continued to build castles. Their complexity and scale continued to grow. His determination and dedication to his creation long outlasted anyone else's interest. I often sat nearby reading. He would call to me, "Hey, Dad, what do you think?" And I would reply, "That's fantastic." Or say, "How about adding some roads?" Or, "Do you think that one needs more turrets?" He would give his opinion and I would end with, "Go for it. I think it looks great!"

This past summer, I noticed a new development on Nanny and Poppy's beach. Dan still works the sand into his creations, but now his four-year-old cousin joins him. As Dan works, he directs his cousin. He shows him how to build moats, turrets, and tunnels. He points out to him weaknesses in his construction. He lends him a hand so his cousin's castles look like Dan's. Often, Dan will say, "That's a good job. It looks great!" Or, "You're doing a great job there." The two of them work side by side, transforming the beach into a myriad of sandcastles.

ACTIVITY: TAKE A MINUTE AND REVIEW THE STORY. WHERE DO YOU SEE THE FOUR M'S AT WORK?

Now how can the four M's help us develop our children's spirituality? At this point you may see that these four parenting modes are helpful to raising a kind and good child, but there is more. When the four M's are tied to the Greatest Commandments given by Jesus, we take on a deeper appreciation of the importance of these parenting modes.

When the lawyer approached Jesus and asked, "Teacher, which commandment in the law is the greatest?" Jesus responded with two commandments. In order to continue my examination of how to help children make good decisions and interact with others, I will begin this section with the second of those commandments. After Jesus answered him, saying, "You shall love the Lord your God, with all your heart, and with all your soul, and with all your mind," he gave his second commandment: "You shall love your neighbor as yourself" (Matt. 22:36-39 NRSV). This simple teaching by Jesus captures the essence of the four M's as they relate to spiritual development in terms of how a child is to make good decisions and interact with others.

As a mirror, parents show children how to love their neighbor by having them reflect on how they would like to be treated. When we patiently show them empathy, remain positive, and build their self-esteem, children in time will learn how to see the impact of their actions and understand the feelings of others.

Jesus' second Great Commandment captures the role of spiritual mentor as well. A mentor is a coach or a guide, so as such, parents look for opportunities to show how children can live out the second Great Commandment. We look for the moments when a child needs a teaching like "love thy neighbor." This can be in simple, ethical teachings about politeness or being considerate of others. It is in the "thank yous" that children learn to love others. When your son or daughter says, "Thank you," it is an opportunity to reinforce this teaching of love.

Moreover, coaching children how to act doesn't stop with simple politeness. How children act on the ball field, with their teachers, and at recess or on the bus matters. Coaching a child how to act remains important into the teenage years. How they treat their boyfriends or girlfriends, and how they treat other drivers on the road, matters. So allowing a child to date doesn't go far enough. He or she must be coached in how to respect and be respected by a boyfriend or girlfriend. Equally, teaching a child how to drive is important, but coaching him or her to respect and honor other drivers is critical, especially when road rage is so rampant. In short, parental teaching doesn't end at kindergarten. Being mindful of Jesus' teaching about neighbors is the foundation of parental spiritual mentoring.

The act of modeling also calls us to heed the second Great Commandment. How do we treat our neighbors? How do we act as spectators at our children's sporting events? How do we act when someone cuts us off in traffic? How do we treat our spouse and children? And even how do we treat our bodies? Since our children scrutinize our actions, what we do matters. Our choices and how we respond in times of stress impacts our children's choices. Therefore, we should take the opportunity as parent-saints to live out "loving our neighbor" more and more and model it for our children.

A parental spiritual motivator stimulates his or her children to understand, follow, and live out "love thy neighbor." We reward good behavior and gently reprove bad behavior. We encourage our children to seek to be kind, generous, and loving to our neighbors, whoever they are. We reprove our children when they treat others poorly. In doing so, we strive for a balance; we remain empathetic to their emotions. And always, we seek to treat our children with respect.

We have looked closely at the second Great Commandment, in which Jesus gave us a practical and simple ethic to make good decisions and successfully interact with others. However, spiritual intelligence involves not just a set of morals. It is also a sense of purpose beyond us, which in Christianity is faith, hope, and trust in God. Turning back to the first Great Commandment—"You shall love the Lord your God"—we see that the four M's are equally important for parental spiritual formation of children. Through the four M's we teach our children not just an ethic, but faith.

We mirror to our children a love of God as we show them his greatness: "How does the beautiful sunset make you feel? Isn't it wonderful how God created the beauty of the world?" or "How did you feel at the Christmas Eve service? What did you think of the story of the baby Jesus?" Mirroring is best done in a positive light, seeking to encourage a sense of wonder and delight in creation, Jesus, and God.

We can coach and guide our children toward a love of God as well. Teach them to say the Lord's Prayer. Say it with them each night. Encourage them to say grace before meals. If you grew up without such spiritual guidance from your parents, it may be awkward at first to engage in these practices with your children. But remember, your children know only what you're doing with them. Your awkwardness will quickly pass.

Praying with your children at bedside or saying a simple grace before a meal models for them how to love God. These actions give your children a sense of purpose outside of themselves. They see these actions that show your faith, hope, and trust in God, and adopt for themselves faith, hope, and trust in God, too.

We grow our children's souls by encouraging them to take actions in which their souls grow. Having everyone take turns saying grace will greatly increase the confidence of not only your children's faith, but yours, too! Having them say their prayers aloud or saying them together will motivate your children to say their own prayers. As I say bedtime prayers for my children, I notice a calm bliss comes over them. They often close their eyes, relax, and feel love. They feel the love I have for them; they feel the love God has for them. They in turn then fold their hands and pray. And once they're done, they open their eyes, seeking my approval. In this nightly ritual, which I have done thousands of times, I have seen their spiritual intelligence increase. It has occurred slowly, drop by drop, but their spiritual wells have deepened and filled with each drop.

Activity One

Imagine your child is walking across the stage to receive his or her high school diploma. After she receives the diploma, she turns to the crowd and makes eye contact with you. Beyond the smiles and the obvious pride or relief, what qualities do you hope your child embodies? List some of these qualities.

The following is a list of Christ-like qualities and attributes that Paul describes in the Book of Romans, chapter 12. Dr. Chester Tolson and Dr. Harold Koenig, M.D., in their book, *The Healing Power of Prayer: The Surprising Connection Between Prayer and Your Health*. Look at this list as a model for your life and for what you should teach your children.

Love without hypocrisy.
Abhor evil.
Cling to the good.
Be kindly and affectionate to one another.
Don't be lazy and let others do all the work.
Try to carry your own burdens.
Be enthusiastic.
Serve the Lord.
Be joyful.
Have hope.
Be patient.

Pray regularly.
Concern yourselves with others' needs.
Give to others.
Be friendly.
Don't hold a grudge.
Bless your enemies.
Rejoice when others are happy.
Mourn with those who mourn.
Don't plan revenge.[28]

Activity Two

How many qualities from the list you made in Activity One coincide with those listed about Christ?

Which Christ-like qualities do you most want to instill in your children?

How can you mirror, mentor, model, or motivate your child to become more Christ-like?

CHAPTER 3 ❧

The Sermon on the Mount: A Parent's Guide to Increasing Your Child's SQ

Happy are those whose greatest desire is to do what God requires; God will satisfy them fully!

(Matt. 5:6 GNT)

The energy and demand of young children is astounding. I still can recall many an afternoon being utterly exhausted from tending the needs of my two children. And even how much more work their mother did! Oh, how I longed for a break from the constant attention that parenting demands. I was very thankful to discover the joy of the ice cream sundae. I would announce, "Do you guys want an ice cream sundae?" My children would squeal with delight. It's funny to think how putting a dirty dish into the dishwasher is a chore, but getting out the ice cream and bowls and spoons is a privilege. As I scooped out each serving and they poured on the chocolate syrup and adorned their creations with whipped cream and candy, a blessed peace would settle over our house. For ten minutes, my children focused all their energy on consuming their cold piles of delight.

Starting in the fifth chapter of Matthew, the Sermon on the Mount opens with the Beatitudes, a series of blessed declarations. The seventh one begins, "Blessed are the peacemakers..." (NRSV). I can't help but think of ice cream sundaes because of the blessed peace they brought to my home.

On a more serious note, most scholars agree that the Sermon on the Mount is one of, if not the, greatest moral teachings we have. Donald Hagner, in his commentary on Matthew's Gospel, writes that the sermon is the "first and main example of the ethical teaching of Jesus."[29] The sermon, which is really a compilation of Jesus' sayings, is the first of five of Jesus' teachings found in the Gospel. Hagner also notes that its placement as the first teaching gives it a "special relevance."[30] Moreover, Raymond E. Brown in his book, *An Introduction to the New Testament*, notes, "Matthew's Sermon on the Mount, the (eight) beatitudes, and the Lord's Prayer are among the most widely known treasures in the Christian heritage."[31] Given its special qualities, this sermon is important for us to explore as an aid in developing our child's SQ.

The Sermon on the Mount is front and center because its teachings put us on the right path. Brown writes that it is "a harmonious masterpiece of ethical and religious teaching."[32] The sermon begins with the Beatitudes, which Brown notes "have been revered for expressing succinctly the values on which Jesus places priority."[33] Following the Beatitudes, Jesus expresses his role as the one who "fulfills" the law and what the Old Testament prophets have foretold. Following his six statements that juxtapose his ethical teachings and the Jewish law, Jesus then, in Chapter Six, defines piety, prayer and how we need to be oriented toward God. In Chapter Seven, Jesus provides more depth to his ethical teaching and the reward of heaven. Step by step, Jesus lays out a clear path of righteous living.

By itself, the Sermon on the Mount provides parents with the pathway to increase their child's SQ. With such sayings as

"Blessed are the merciful, for they will receive mercy" (Matt. 5:7 NRSV), "Let your word be 'Yes, Yes' or 'No, No'" (Matt. 5:37 NRSV), and "Why do you see the speck in you neighbor's eye, but do not notice the log in your own eye" (Matt. 7:3 NRSV), parents can mentor their child. The attitudes of generosity, mercy, and kindness that infuse the sermon help provide a firm ethical foundation. Moreover, the teachings on piety and prayer give parents the tools for modeling solid, religious habits. Drawing upon these three chapters that make up the Sermon, parents can teach their children how to live good lives.

At this point, you may be asking, "But aren't there more of Jesus' teachings in the Bible?" Yes, there are many more teaching sections, not just in the New Testament, but also in the whole Bible, that give guidance for how to live a good life. In fact, the Sermon on the Mount is just one of five teachings in the Gospel of Matthew. The other three Gospels also contain many of Jesus' teachings. Sometimes a teaching is found in all four Gospels and other times it is found in only one. At times, similar teachings seem to contradict each other. In looking at similar teachings, confusion often arises in the heart of the reader.

In light of potential contradiction and confusion, how does one approach biblical teachings? First, Sandra Schneiders writes in *The Revelatory Text: Interpreting the New Testament as Sacred Scripture* that "words change meaning over time," "no language is fully translatable," and "language is finite."[34] And in contrast to language, God is ageless and has no boundaries. So our words, while giving us the amazing ability to describe our encounters with the divine, fall short. Words and language cannot fully describe God. Thus there are places in the Bible where contradictions arise. These are due in part to the finiteness of human language and understanding.

It is important to keep this in mind as one reads the Bible. On the one hand, the Bible is a historical account of how God has interacted with individuals and peoples, especially the Israelites.

account reminded and interpreted for the Israelites
ways God encountered human beings. It revealed God's
gs in the world. In this way, the Bible is revelation.

ut the Bible is not a past, static revelation. It is more.
Schneiders writes that the Bible is "(potentially) revelatory"[35]
for the reader today. When a reader approaches the Bible with
faith, he or she suddenly enters into a medium where he or she
can encounter God. (For some readers, this statement was just
a big leap of faith in itself!) Let me break it down. Most simply,
faith is belief, hope, and trust in God. Hebrews 11 begins, "Now
faith is the assurance of things hoped for, the conviction of things
not seen" (NRSV). Faith is an openness and willingness to trust
a God we cannot see or touch.

When we read the Bible with faith, we allow the stories and
lessons in it to affect us. In answering a question about how her
view of Jesus changed after she read the Gospel of Mark, one of
my confirmation students responded: "After reading of (Jesus')
amazing life, I feel that I know him much more. Instead of being
a strange and distant figure in heaven I now feel as if he is an
eternal presence and even a friend sent to guide us through life."
Her words represent the effect of revelation. For her, the Bible
is not simply a treasured story. It is more, because she now feels
Jesus' presence. This effect is the divine encounter. The Bible's
language shapes our minds, and we are changed by it.

Following are several dialogues between different parents and
their pastors. They outline several parenting problems and how
the pastors respond by drawing from the teachings in the Sermon
on the Mount. Notice how the teachings inform and reform the
parents and bring out new ways to parent their children.

Dialogue One

Keith and Jenny Johnson sit down with Father David. They
are distraught about the way their two sons keep fighting with
each other.

Father David: Keith and Jenny, I am glad we have this chance to meet. Tell me what's going on at home.

Jenny: As you may have noticed, Drew (9) and Peter (7) are always fighting. It's been bad for a while, but recently it seems to be getting worse. Friday, while the boys were walking home together from the bus, Drew punched Peter in the stomach. It took the wind out of Peter. Mrs. Franklin, our neighbor, saw the whole thing. That's the only reason we knew about it.

Keith: I thought this was just boys being boys. My brothers and I were always roughhousing. My mother hated it. We were always breaking something. But there seems to be more to Drew's anger toward Peter. When I talked to Drew about it, he was remorseless. He apologized when I threatened to take away his video game system, but he didn't mean it.

Jenny: I asked him if there was something wrong at school, but he said no and walked away. I feel like he is shutting us out.

Father David: Well, experience tells me that there is more going on with Drew than we know. I wonder what happens to Drew on the bus.

Keith: Peter did say to me that some of the kids on the bus tease Drew. He is the quieter of our two. Peter always makes friends easily.

Father David: Sounds like the problem is bullying and jealousy. The Bible has many stories and lessons about bullying and jealousy—you may recall that jealousy starts early in the Bible with Cain and Abel. And Jesus gives us several teachings about it in the Sermon on the Mount. In Chapter 5, verse 22, Jesus says, "I say to you that if you are angry with your brother or sister, you will be liable to judgment ... if you remember that your brother or sister has something against you, leave your gift before the altar and go; first be reconciled to your brother and sister." What Jesus says here is we cannot receive his forgiveness if we are angry with, in this case, our brother. Drew and Peter need to speak to each other, in your presence, and share their feelings.

Keith: Father, that is easier said than done. These are young boys.

Father David: I agree with you. This may be very difficult for them, but encourage them to speak about their feelings. Teach them that this is what God expects of them. God doesn't want them to be angry at each other. The blessing of this teaching is that it forces us to recognize that God, the creator of the uNIVerse, expects us to live a certain way.

Jenny: You mean the Golden Rule.

Father David: Exactly. Later in the Sermon, Chapter 7, verse 12, Jesus says, "In everything do to others as you would have them do to you." All of us need constant reminding of this lesson. It is hard to live this way, but by doing so Drew can face his jealousy toward Peter, and Peter can face how his popularity hurts his brother.

Keith: What does the Bible say about bullying?

Father David: Well, the Sermon gives us a tough lesson. It is a lesson on how to stop the cycle of violence. Bullying often develops out of a cycle of oppression, hatred, jealousy, and the like. A parent can be abusing a child, and the child might turn around and hurt another child as an outlet. Or one child, usually an older child, teases another child who in turn teases another younger child. Bullying will only stop if the cycle is broken.

Keith: So what does Jesus say?

Father David: In the Sermon, Chapter 5, verses 38-48, Jesus says, "You have heard that it was said, 'An eye for an eye and a tooth for a tooth.' But I say to you, 'Do not resist an evildoer. But if anyone strikes you on the right cheek, turn the other also.'" Then he says, "You have heard it said, 'You shall love your neighbor and hate your enemy.' But I say to you, 'Love your enemies and pray for those who persecute you, so that you may be children of your Father in heaven.'" Jesus is very perceptive

about human nature. He is saying that we cannot control the
actions of others, but we can control how we respond. Drew
cannot stop the person from teasing him, because he cannot
control the other person. Except, of course, unless Drew chooses
to fight the bully, but that usually ends with Drew in trouble, too.
So the better course is for Drew to turn the other cheek, which
is to ignore it. And to pray for the person who is bullying him.
In other words, bring God into the picture. By praying, Drew
will acknowledge who is bothering him and will see the bully
for who he or she is—a person who is troubled and insecure in
some way. God will give him direction, which may come from
you listening to his prayer.

Dialogue Two

Scott and Grace Allen are meeting with Mother Claire. They
are concerned about the way their daughter constantly speaks
about her peers.

Mother Claire: It is so good to see you. How have you been,
and how is Suzanne?

Grace: Well, Suzanne is the reason we're here.

Mother Claire: Really? What's the problem?

Scott: She has been very negative toward her classmates and
friends.

Grace: She is constantly gossiping about them and putting
them down.

Mother Claire: Sounds like she is being very judgmental.

Both: Yes.

Mother Claire: Well, the Bible gives us lots advice about
these things. In fact, Jesus was very clear about judging others
toward the end of the Sermon on the Mount. He says, "Do not
judge, so that you may not be judged. For with the judgment
you make you will be judged, and the measure you give will be
the measure you get." Then he continues, "Why do you see the
speck in your neighbor's eye but do not notice the log in your

own eye? Or how can you say to your neighbor, 'Let me take the speck out of your eye' while the log is in your own eye?" What do you think Jesus is saying here?

Scott: My mother used to always say, "Don't worry about the speck in your friend's eye because you have a log in your eye." She would always say that when I got critical about my friends. It would help me have empathy toward my friends and remember that I wasn't perfect.

Mother Claire: Right. Jesus wants us to remember that we are sinners—not perfect—and that we make mistakes. By remembering our own fallen nature, we become less judgmental of others. We also become more patient with people.

Scott: Boy, I need to remember that.

Grace: You sure do.

Mother Claire: Okay. Let's not get judgmental. Generally what bothers us about others is a weakness within ourselves. That is why Jesus uses "speck" and "log." Our greatest failings can be areas where we quickly find fault in others, even if it is only a minor flaw in the other person.

Grace: So what do we do about Suzanne?

Mother Claire: I want you to start by reflecting on how you act around her. Are you on the phone gossiping and being negative about your friends? Do you come home from work and complain about your coworkers? Do you gripe about your neighbors? If you do, remember Suzanne may be modeling your actions. Then you need to mentor her, just like Scott's mother used to do with Scott. Those little sayings stay with us. They are easy to remember. The Sermon on the Mount is full of those little one-liners. Jesus taught with them because they are so easy to remember.

Activity

Read the Sermon on the Mount in Matthew 5–7. As you do, think about your children. What teaching from the Sermon applies to your children and how it would benefit them.

The Sermon on the Mount: A Parent's Guide to Increasing Your Child's SQ

The Sermon on the Mount holds such importance because it's the first of Jesus' teachings. Also, it is practical. It addresses real-life situations that are innate to human nature. Teachings about how to live with other people, being honest, being tolerant, keeping God as the center of one's life, and how to pray are worthy lessons as applicable to twenty-first century life as they were in the first century. Moreover, even though not all biblical lessons may apply to our lives, their moral teachings are sound. For instance, one may not have to grapple with divorce in his or her own marriage, but Jesus' teachings on divorce help a reader understand the weight and importance that God has regarding the institution.

When one looks to the Bible for moral lessons, one does so understanding that some teachings may not fit all present circumstances. But others will and do. So one reads the Bible with sensitivity, looking for those lessons that affect him or her and bring out the best in parents and children. It is imperative that one reads the Bible knowing that it can have an effect. It can and does change the reader and immensely helps parents to successfully develop a child's SQ. Bible reading is an essential pathway for parents and children to live righteous and good lives.

CHAPTER 4 ❧

Developing Rituals: Habits That Help Form Your Child's SQ

God prefers bad verses recited with a pure heart, to the finest verses possible chanted by the wicked.

(Voltaire, *The Works of Voltaire*)[36]

I don't recall exactly when my mother first taught me to pray, but I know she did. My first memory of her helping me pray was at bedtime, when she would read from my illustrated Bible. It was the King James Version with red letters highlighting when Jesus was speaking and fabulously detailed colored drawings of special stories and events in the Scriptures. I have that Bible still, but I cannot read its Edwardian "thy" and "thou" for very long. What a relief to discover as an adult the many different translations of the Bible!

What I do remember is my mother helping me find the Twenty-third Psalm. I don't remember why I wanted to find it or if she pointed me toward it. Lying in the comfort of my sheets, all tucked in for the night and surrounded by soft-hued light, I found comfort in those words. How old was I, I wonder?

Maybe seven or eight. I was young, but even in my innocence those fifteen lines were a balm to my soul.

In his book, *The Lord Is My Shepherd: Healing Wisdom of the Twenty-Third Psalm*, Rabbi Harold S. Kushner writes, "Can fifteen beautiful lines from a single page of the Bible change your life? I believe they can."[37] He goes on to describe the Twenty-third Psalm this way: "In just a few lines, it conveys the distilled wisdom of generations, offering us a way of seeing the world that renders it less frightening, teaching us to deal with the loss of people we love and with conflict with people who don't like us or treat us badly. It shows us how to recognize the presence of God at times and in places where we might think God was absent or when we might be so distracted by our own concerns that we would overlook God's presence."[38] I couldn't agree more. Every night for many years I went to my Bible, until I knew the prayer by heart, and prayed the Twenty-third Psalm. Because of my nightly ritual, I drifted off to sleep full of courage and hope, and assured of God's presence in my life.

Loehr and Schwartz describe rituals as "precise, consciously acquired behaviors that become automatic in our lives".[39] They point to a "growing body of research" that "suggests that as little as five percent of our behaviors are consciously self-directed."[40] They continue, "We are creatures of habit and as much as 95 percent of what we do occurs automatically or in reaction to a demand or an anxiety."[41] Therefore, if we want to develop a child's SQ, we can do so by establishing rituals or habits that become automatic in their lives, so when difficulties arise they will have a well of habits and rituals from which to draw that will give them purpose, strength, comfort, and hope. Loehr and Schwartz add, "Rituals serve as anchors, ensuring that even in the most difficult circumstances we will continue to use our energy in service of the values that we hold most dear."[42]

Dr. Scott Peck's famous opening line from *The Road Less Traveled* is, "Life is difficult."[43] And so true it is. Life's difficult circumstances are often described as storms. Our personal storms come in as many varieties as storms occurring in nature. Our storms feel at times like Category Five hurricanes, F-5 tornadoes, and 7.5 magnitude earthquakes.

The Bible is full of people dealing with and reacting to storms of all kinds. The storm Jesus and his disciples encountered while crossing the Sea of Galilee, for example, illustrates how people tend to act in crises. Jesus wanted to cross the Sea of Galilee. He got into a boat and his disciples boarded, too. Soon after they set sail, Jesus fell asleep. The Gospel of Matthew says that a windstorm arose on the sea. It was so great that the boat was being swamped by the waves. We can imagine the distress besetting the disciples, who were still new to Jesus' ministry and mission. Jesus, having healed and cured countless people over the last days and nights, was sleeping. The disciples knew he was tired, but their habit was to seek Jesus' advice and leadership at all times—especially in difficult ones. So instead of trusting their own faith and gathering in prayer for help and saving, they woke Jesus. Jesus, in turn, chastised them for not handling the storm by their own exhortation and prayer. And then he quieted the wind by rebuking it. Beyond recognizing Jesus' amazing power, the story points out that early in their ministry and mission the disciples turned to Jesus for help in a crisis. Later in the Gospel of Matthew, we see the more "independent" disciples handle challenges in different ways. One way of reading not only Matthew's Gospel, but the other three as well, is to see how Jesus develops and strengthens the faith of those around him, especially the disciples.

Like Jesus' leadership in developing and strengthening his followers' faith, the most important thing we can do as parents is to instill in our children spiritual rituals that develop and strengthen their faith. Over time with repetition, spiritual rituals become habits. With basic spiritual habits in place, our children will be able to better weather their lives' storms. They will have rituals or basic habits on which they can rely to bring them purpose, strength, comfort, and hope.

Basic Habits

There are three basic habits or rituals through which we actively develop our own and our children's SQs: praying, reading the Bible, and attending church services. Can it be that simple? Yes!

These three activities are simple, but it takes work and repetition to develop them into daily habits. Having grown up in New England, I take seriously my desire for private prayer. For many years I was loath to bow my head in prayer anywhere but in church or in the privacy of my bedroom. I remember the first time I paused to quietly say grace before a workday lunch. I was in a McDonald's on Route 1 in Mamaroneck, New York. I had a salad and a diet Coke. I sat in a quiet alcove where only a couple of other people were eating lunch—they were five tables away from me and engrossed in a conversation. I bowed my head and thanked God for my food. I think if someone had come up to me and asked me if I was praying, I would have dropped dead of embarrassment right then and there.

I wonder why it's so difficult to stop and pray or read the Bible or get up on a Sunday morning to go to church? There is an initial inertia that holds us back. Maybe the answer is utilitarian. If we don't see the benefit, then why expend the energy to create a new habit? Well, there are benefits to each basic habit that are beyond the aid they provide during the pounding waves of life's storms. Dr. Harold Koenig notes in his book, *The Healing Power of Faith: How Belief and Prayer Can Help You Triumph Over Disease*, that there are many benefits attributed to faith, and especially prayer. Dr. Koenig, who is a professor of psychiatry and behavioral sciences and associate professor of medicine at

Duke University Medical Center, writes that Duke's Center for the Study of Religion/Spirituality and Health has found that "people who regularly attend church, pray individually, and read the Bible have significantly lower diastolic blood pressure than the less religious."[44] Additionally, people who "attend church regularly are hospitalized much less often."[45] Also, "people who attend religious services regularly have stronger immune systems than their less religious counterparts."[46] His list of benefits due to the three basic religious habits goes on to include life longevity, stronger marriages, and stress reduction. So there is a great benefit to spiritual practices, even at a McDonald's. And if we are to develop daily habits in our children, we must develop them in ourselves, too.

Habit One: Prayer

Stripped down to its most basic form, function, and fashion, prayer is the act of speaking with God. This act involves our thoughts, silently or aloud, and our pausing for a response. Prayer is simple.

That said, conversing with the Creator of the uNIverse can be intimidating. How do we form the words that take our most basic, pedestrian needs and make them worthy of God Almighty's attention? You might be saying, "God has better things to do in his day than listen to my pitiful concerns." Fortunately, we have pre-written prayers, many of which are ancient, that we can use in our conversations with God. Here are some of my favorites:

The Lord is my Shepherd;
I shall not want.
He maketh me lie down in green pastures;
He leadeth me beside still waters.
He restoreth my soul;
He leadeth me in the paths of righteousness for his

Name's sake.
Yea, though I walk through the valley of the shadow of
death,
I will fear no evil; for thou art with me;
Thy rod and thy staff, they comfort me,
Thou preparest a table before me in the presence of my
enemies;
Thou anointest my head with oil;
My cup runneth over.
Surely goodness and mercy shall follow me all the days of
my life,
And I will dwell in the house of the Lord for ever. (Psalm
23 KJV)

The Lord's Prayer
Our Father, who art in heaven,
hallowed be thy Name,
thy kingdom come,
thy will be done,
on earth as it is in heaven.
Give us this day our daily bread
And forgive us our trespasses,
As we forgive those who trespass against us.
And lead us not into temptation,
but deliver us from evil.
For thine is the kingdom and the power,
and the glory, for ever and ever. Amen.[47]

Prayer of St. Francis
Lord, make me an instrument of your peace.
Where there is hatred, let me sow love;
Where there is injury, pardon,
Where there is doubt, faith,
Where there is despair, hope,
Where there is darkness, light,
and where there is sadness, joy.
O Divine Master, grant that I may

not so much seek to be consoled, as to console;
To be understood, as to understand;
To be loved, as to love;
For it is in giving that we receive –
It is in pardoning that we are pardoned;
And it is in dying that we are born to eternal life.[48]

A Child's Bedtime Prayer
Now I lay me down to sleep,
I pray the Lord my soul to keep.
Watch over me the starry night,
And wake me in the morning light.

Several themes run through these prayers. One is recognizing God in our lives. Another is that we are God's possession. Still another is our need for God's help. And in each prayer there is hope that after our death we will be with God in heaven. These prayers give us strength, courage, comfort, and hope.

Moreover, our speaking with God is not limited to the words that our forbearers used. We can converse freely and openly with God, but if we want to find a middle ground between written prayers and ordinary conversing, we can use simple mnemonic aid. There are several different mnemonic aids; the one I like is PATH. Each letter represents a word that is an appropriate form of prayer. "P" stands for "Praise." Starting off a prayer by praising God turns our focus on God. Praising God makes us think about what God has done for us. Praising God lifts our hearts and attitudes; it begins to fill our spiritual well. It causes our thoughts to rise into light and goodness. It gives us a heavenly view.

Next is "A," which stands for "Acknowledgment." We acknowledge to God all the ways we have fallen short: the wrongs we have said, the sins we have committed, and the things we have forgotten.

Then we move on to "T" and "Thanksgivings." We thank God for all the blessings of our lives. We thank God for the good things we have received from him and from other people.

The final letter, "H," stands for "Help." After praising God, acknowledging our wrongs, and thanking God for our blessings, we ask God for help. We pray for guidance, healing, blessing, intervention, protection, etc. Here we open our hearts up to our loving God who in his great mercy hears our vulnerable calls for help.

PATH puts us on the right path to God. It helps us remember our role in relating to God. It gives us a format for approaching God in personal prayer that is open and flexible, fitting into our own personal style. With each step along the PATH our spiritual wells fill. God's Spirit pours life-giving water into our clear, cool pool of spiritual energy.

Activity One

Using the PATH technique, write a prayer for your child to use.
Name three words you can use to praise God.
Name the wrongdoings your child often commits.
Describe things for which your child can give thanks to God.
Ask God's help.

For the last ten years, my nightly ritual has included blessing each of my children. I began doing it long before I became a priest. Now my children often say, "Dad, I need my blessing." I recommend blessing your children each night. What I say comes from Numbers 6:24-27:

> May the Lord bless you and keep you.
> May he turn his head toward you and be gracious to you.
> May he shine his face upon you and give you peace.

Then I add these words from *The Book of Common Prayer*.
Guide us waking, O Lord, and guard us sleeping.
That awake we may watch with Christ,
And asleep we may rest in peace.[49]

I also strongly encourage you to say grace at each meal.
Again, a simple prayer of one or two sentences is sufficient.
It does a couple of things. It causes everyone to start the meal
together. That is simple politeness. If we don't, the one who
cooked the meal is usually the last one to eat. It promotes respect
of elders. Children, who have done nothing to provide or prepare
the meal and devour the food before the adults have sat, tend
to lose respect of the same adults who provide for them. Grace
also causes us to pause and remember that the sun, rain, and
soil are God-given gifts that provide the food we eat. Here are
a couple of graces that I often use:

> Bless us, O Lord, for these thy gifts we are about to receive,
> in Jesus Christ's name we pray. Amen.

> Bless this food to our use and us to thy service, in Jesus'
> name. Amen.

> God is great. God is good. And we thank him for our food.
> By his hands, we all are fed. Give us forth our daily bread.
> Amen.

> Thank You, Lord, for this food and the loving hands that
> prepared it. May it nourish and sustain us. Amen.

The great Roman Catholic nun, Mother Teresa of Calcutta,
left us simple but profound advice about prayer: "Start and end
the day with prayer. Come to God as a child. ... When you pray,
give thanks to God for all his gifts because everything is his and

a gift from him. (Even) your soul is a gift of God."[50] Then she urges us at the end of the day to self examine our day and to say, "I'm very sorry" to God for all our wrongs, and commit to living better tomorrow.[51]

God doesn't want profound prayers. He just wants to hear from us. We should teach our children that checking in with God each day is vital. Doing so will free them from worry, guilt, and despair, and they will gain strength, courage, comfort, and hope.

Habit Two: Bible Reading

One of the most admired people of the twentieth century, the evangelist Rev. Dr. Billy Graham, writes in his book, *Peace with God*, about guidelines for Christian living. He places Bible reading as our most important activity. He writes, "First: you should read your Bible daily. It is one of your greatest privileges. Your spiritual life needs food. What kind of food? Spiritual food. Where do you find this spiritual food? In the Bible, the Word of God."[52] Building the habit of Bible reading is critical for SQ development.

Fortunately, today's children don't have to tackle the King James Version of the Bible just to become familiar with the Bible. Major bookstore retailers and online sellers provide parents with many quality Bibles that are age appropriate. For many years, my son read *The Beginner's Bible: Timeless Children's Stories* by Kelly Pulley. One day, he announced with great pride, "I've read the Bible three times!" The great things about this Bible were each page was illustrated and it covered all the major Bible stories, so my son was able to learn the foundational stories of Christianity. By reading the Bible, children affirm their innate feeling and belief that God is a natural part of human life experience. It gives context and shape to their deep-seated religious nature. It increases their SQ.

Activity Two

Take a field trip to your local bookstore. Take your child with you and look over the Bibles in the religious section. Or go online and do the same.

Another form of Bible reading is devotionals. This is a very popular, personal Christian activity. There are many devotionals available, written by many people. Oswald Chambers' *My Utmost for His Highest* is one of the classic devotional books and a favorite of mine. The devotional book format is simple. Each book includes a series of devotionals, for a month, a year, or somewhere in between. Each devotional begins with a short Bible verse. Then the author adds a short commentary. Sometimes the commentaries are followed by one or more questions or a prayer. You can use these devotionals as a daily anchor to guide your thoughts and intentions for that day.

Devotionals are very important. A recent study showed that family devotional practice is often the best predictor of a child's frequent, regular church attendance as an adult. The second half of this book includes a series of family devotionals that I have written especially for you. They are organized in the typical format and include questions for you and your children to discuss. I strongly encourage you to use these devotionals and look for others after you have completed them.

Activity Three

Read a devotional with your children. Turn to Part II and pick out a devotional. During dinner or at bedtime, read the devotional aloud to your child and discuss the questions.

Habit Three: Attending Church

In his book, *Here and Now: Living in the Spirit*, beloved and gifted author Henri Nouwen writes, "We cannot live a spiritual life alone."[53] He continues, "It is very hard to live a life of prayer in a milieu where no one prays or speaks lovingly about prayer. It is nearly impossible to deepen our communion with God when those with whom we live and work reject or even ridicule the idea that there is a loving God."[54] Nouwen's words are perfect. In our culture where Christian symbols are under assault and where many people feel hesitant to even wish someone a "Merry Christmas" for fear of offending a person's beliefs, it is difficult to deepen one's spiritual well without the support of a community of believers (i.e., the church). Regular worship is important to our and our children's spiritual development.

Many people have said to me, "I don't like the institutional church" or "I had a bad experience once." Still others have said, "Everyone in church is a hypocrite" or even, "I am spiritual but not religious." All of these statements and the stories that go with them show the pain that can come with going to church, but they are excuses nonetheless. Years ago, I was having difficulty with a co-leader of a church youth group. I was so frustrated that I wanted to drop out of the group's leadership team and not come to church for a while. When I told the priest, she said to me, "Don't let anyone keep you from God." She was right. I was letting another person stand in the way of my relationship with God.

Church teaches us about God. Church fortifies us to live the Christian life in an increasingly secular world. Church gives us moral strengthening. It reminds us that there is a greater force in the uNIVerse than ourselves. It gives us hope. And the Church is a community of believers. But as Henri Nouwen writes in *Making All Things New: an Invitation to the Spiritual Life*, the Church "community has little to do with mutual compatibility."[55] The Church community has less to do with "similarities in educational background, psychological make-up, or social status";[56] it is about God. It is "grounded in God, who calls us together."[57] Nouwen's lesson is important not just for our children to learn, but also for us to remember. Church is a human institution and comes with what makes us best and worst.

In spite of the difficulty of loving our neighbor—in the next pew—attending church is vitally important. From the physical benefits of lowering one's blood pressure and stress level and promoting longevity, to giving us a moral compass, a purpose for life, and a connection to God, the Church provides you and your children with many, many benefits.

FINAL THOUGHTS

These three habits are the same for the beginning Christian as they are for the most spiritual monk or nun. The difference between the "novice" and the "professional" is only a matter of practice or discipline. Developing these habits in our children allows them to develop a deep enough spiritual energy well to aid them in illness and crises.

I am reminded of a woman I met while working as a hospital chaplain. Before I went into her room, I was told that she was poor, mentally disabled, and her family lived several hours from the hospital, meaning she was alone. She had very advanced cancer; she was dying. The nurses on the unit asked me to see her because they couldn't control her pain (an unusual occurrence these days). I went in. We spoke through her pain. I found the only thing that lessened her yelling and moaning was prayer. She knew the Lord's Prayer. So we prayed it together.

Our children need to know prayers and the Bible, and they need to develop their spirituality through church service attendance—because in their desperate hours, it is only God who can give them comfort and peace. In addition, these habits will cause them to be healthier people who have better relationships and less stress. Oh, yes: they may live longer, too.

CHAPTER 5 ❧

Introducing Your Child to Communion

The Gifts of God for the People of God. Take them in remembrance that Christ died for you, and feed on him in your hearts by faith, with thanksgiving.

(*The Book of Common Prayer*)[58]

One Sunday after church, my wife and I approached our priest to ask when our then-seven-year-old daughter could—or rather "should"—receive Communion. Father George said he would know when it was the right time. He always had a sense of when a child was ready to receive Communion. At the time, I was relieved to know he was cognizant of the preparedness of the children who came to the altar rail. But I was also uneasy. Shouldn't she have some instruction? Shouldn't she be made aware how special and important Communion is? Shouldn't she understand the implicit etiquette? His explanation left me mystified about a priest's intuitive awareness and curious about the relationship between children, God, and their readiness to receive Communion.

As someone who now stands on the other side of the altar rail and distributes the body and blood of Christ, I appreciate Father George's teaching. However, I feel that children need instruction about Communion. The purpose of this chapter is to give parents a basic theological understanding of Communion. In reading this chapter, it is important for you to be aware that I write this from my own perspective and theological training. I have been an Episcopalian since I was five and I am grounded in the Protestant side of my denomination. So if in reading this chapter you find a different understanding of Communion, I suggest that you speak to your pastor. Use this material as a jumping off point to deepen your own theological understanding of Communion as it is expressed in your denomination.

Some children who come forward, kneel, and extend their hands to share in the body of Christ seem to have an intuitive understanding. This understanding may develop for a variety of reasons. They may simply want to be partakers with the community. They may want to feel that they too can "sit at the table and dine with God." Or they may feel the lure of the Spirit drawing them into the relationship with God that is open to all who are baptized. For whatever reason, when I see little hands unfolded to receive the body of Christ, I know that they do so because they want to partake and share in the mystery that is Communion. And I am privileged to witness the consummation of a relationship that will last a lifetime.

As parents, we are called to instill in our children the basic theological tenets of the Communion through instruction. We teach our children about why the moments at the altar rail are so special, meaningful, and mysterious. In doing so, we give our children a very important and special tool for increasing their SQ. The active presence of God in church, and especially in the bread and wine, will transform them, and the relationship creates the core foundation of SQ. God's presence in the bread and wine will alter them in a way that deepens their spiritual wells. In those moments of Communion with the Creator of the uNIVerse, God becomes personal and so close that his presence can be felt in the space between each strand of our DNA's double helix.

The following story illustrates the different parts of the Communion. After the story, I will explain how children can understand each part.

ON OUR KNEES

Bobby's knees hit the cushion with a thump that moves the kneeler forward until it slides under the pew in front of us. It bumps into Mr. Jenkins' feet. Mr. Jenkins wiggles a bit and I softly say, "Sorry." I want to scold Bobby but he has already moved his kneeler back and folded his hands in prayer and, to my surprise, seems to be listening intently to the minister as he begins the prayer.

The minister says, "The Lord be with you." And everyone, including Bobby and me, replies, "And also with you." We've been coming to church more and more these days. I think it is a good thing for Bobby to experience. While he fidgets during the sermon, often coloring or drawing, he seems to carefully listen to the Communion prayer. I think he is curious.

Bobby whispers, "Daddy, why is it right to give God thanks?"

"Well, listen to the minister," I reply. "He is about to tell us."

Bobby closes his eyes and listens and remembers what he was taught in Church School. "Oh, because God created heaven and earth, even me!"

I put my finger to my lips, hoping he will quiet down. Then the organ begins to play and everyone sings, "Holy, holy, holy…"

Bobby pokes my arm. "Daddy, are we praising God, now?"

I nod my head.

Bobby nods back and joins in the singing. I am surprised how quickly he has memorized the response and music.

The organ stops and the minister continues with the prayer. At the word *sin*, Bobby pokes me. He shows me a sad face. I point forward toward the minister. But Bobby interrupts me again.

"Daddy," he whispers, "why did Jesus die?"

I whisper back, "Because God loves us so much."

He nods his head affirmatively. I am frustrated now. As usual, Bobby has completely pulled me away from any sense of holiness.

Bobby pokes me and points toward the altar. This is his favorite part.

The minister continues, "On the night he was handed over to suffering and death, our Lord Jesus Christ took bread…" The minister lifts the bread. I glance at Bobby, who looks up at me. He mouths, "The bread of heaven." Quickly, his attention is back to the minister, who consecrates the bread and wine. Bobby is very intrigued by the minister's hand motions.

We say the Lord's Prayer. Bobby knows this prayer by heart and prays it with his eyes shut tight. Then the minister breaks the consecrated bread. The minister lifts the cup and bread and says, "The gifts of God for the people of God. Take them in remembrance that Christ died for you, and feed on him in your hearts by faith with thanksgiving."

The church springs into action. The organ plays. The ushers move down the aisle. Some people stand, others sit, and still others kneel in thoughtful prayer. We patiently wait our turn.

Bobby asks me, "Daddy, what do you pray about while we are waiting to go up for Communion?"

I tell him I pray that I will grow closer to God, become a better person, remember Jesus' sacrifice, and I give thanks for our family, our health, and everything else God provides. By my prayer I ready myself for Communion.

Bobby nods and knowingly whispers, "That's what my Church School teacher taught me to do, too."

It's our turn now. Bobby stands in line in front of me and behind Mr. Jenkins. We kneel at the altar rail. Bobby looks up at Mr. Jenkins. They make eye contact and smile at each other. Then Mr. Jenkins extends his hands. Bobby does the same, straining his neck to see the minister.

The minister places the consecrated bread in Bobby's hands, saying, "The body of Christ, the bread of heaven." Bobby replies aloud, "Amen." Then he brings his hands to his mouth and eats his piece of the Body of Christ. Although we have never spoken about it, he always waits patiently for me to finish before he moves. He somehow understands that he is to wait. If I asked him, he would say, "It's the polite thing to do."

We go back to our pew, kneel, and say the closing prayer. The final hymn plays. The minister dismisses us and we begin to exit. Bobby and Mr. Jenkins chat. Bobby likes his tie. We greet the minister, who shakes Bobby's hand.

So what happened in this story? Most church services that include Communion or the Lord's Supper are divided into parts. The order of the parts may differ from denomination to denomination, but differences represent local customs or denominational practices. The underlying purpose remains the same in all Christian churches.

The first part happens when the minister says a prayer. At many churches, this prayer is said while people kneel, while at others it is customary for people to stand. Central to the prayer is remembering the core story of the Christian faith: Jesus' last supper, the final hours of his life, his death, and resurrection. What is important for us to teach our children is the reason we remember this story: because of our sin, God had to send Jesus to save us from our sin. Our children need to learn that because of the sinful, bad things we do, we are separated from God. And that it is only because Jesus died for us that we can be with God again. In addition to our remembering the story of salvation, we need to teach our children that Jesus' followers wrote down Jesus' life story and his teachings, and started the Church. Church people such as the ministers (pastors and priests) and others tell the story each week so all of us can know about Jesus.

The prayer is not the only action taking place during this part of the service. In some churches there are a lot of actions like bowing, burning of incense, bell ringing, more bowing, and hand gestures. At other churches very few of these actions take place. At most church services, toward the end of the long prayer, the minister often will make hand motions over the bread and the wine (or in some denominations, grape juice). The minister does this to make the bread and wine special and separate. This action is considered the act of consecration. The bread and wine become the body and blood of Christ. We don't know how this happens; it's a mystery. But we know Jesus is truly present in the bread so we can unite with God. The bread and wine are signs of God's love for us.

There is one more significant action ministers perform. Once the bread is consecrated, the minister breaks the bread. He or she breaks it so we all may share in it. In sharing the bread, we recognize that everyone at the service is a member of Jesus' family. Additionally, the broken bread is a symbol of the breaking of Jesus' body on the cross and of our own sinfulness and need for Jesus to bring us to God.

In my church, when I have finished praying the long prayer that I know as the Communion Prayer, I lift the bread and wine off the table and present them to the congregation. I say, "The gifts of God for the people of God. Take them in remembrance that Christ died for you and feed on him in your heart by faith with thanksgiving." These two sentences can be very helpful for parents. We can explain to our children that the first sentence reminds us the bread is a gift from God in that the sun, rain, and grain, which make the wheat for the bread, all come from God's creation. The same is true for the wine. The second sentence reminds us that in eating the bread and drinking the wine, we remember Jesus died for us. Also, we teach our children that while eating the bread, in our hearts we trust in God, hope for heaven, and give thanks to God for Jesus.

There is one more important symbol we can teach our children about Communion. Denominations have different practices when it comes to receiving, eating, and drinking the holy elements. At some churches, people leave their seats and come forward to an altar rail and kneel in order to receive Communion. At other churches, people come forward and stand in front of the minister. At still other churches, people remain in their seats and the elements are passed one to another and then once everyone has received the elements everyone eats and drinks at the same time. Again, this is a matter of local custom or denominational practice. It is not how or where we receive the elements that is important; it is that we do so in a respectful manner. And it is important to emphasize to our children that this holy moment is a very personal time, but equally it is a public act where our church family comes together as a sign of unity.

Activity One

How is Communion meaningful to you?
Thinking back to the story, which element is most meaningful to you? Why?

THEOLOGICAL THEMES

Communion is the beating heart of our Christian faith. It is a ritual rich in meaning and significance. I liken it to an onion. We can peel back layer after layer, and each layer is as important as the next. The importance of theology in considering Communion is that theology can be "*aids* to faith."[59] So what theological themes can we, as parents, teach our children? Here are a few: Jesus' sacrifice, the real presence, faith and thanksgiving, and the unity of the community. Each theme was touched on in the story. By understanding Communion better, you can nurture your child's Spiritual Intelligence. You can help him or her grow closer to God through the sacred act of eating the holy bread and drinking the holy wine.

Jesus' death on the cross is considered atonement. In the Communion prayer we hear atonement explained as the forgiveness of our sins and reconciliation of us to God. On the cross, Jesus was a perfect sacrifice for the whole world. When we celebrate Communion, we do not repeat what happened on the cross but rather proclaim Christ's sacrificial work on the cross and make present the benefits of the atonement.[60] What are the benefits? In Jesus' atoning work, sinful humanity is reconciled with God. Christ's death on the cross mends our broken relationship with God. So it is through Jesus' sacrifice that we are brought back into a full relationship with God.[61]

Though I cannot explain it fully, Jesus is really present in the bread and wine; not that they materially or physically change, but that Christ's power to transform us is present. I can argue that Christ is present anytime that two or three gather for worship, as in the Prayer of St. Chrysostom,[62] but to simply leave it at that undercuts the power of Communion. Presence means Jesus' power to transform us from sinners to a relationship with God is available for all those who in faith receive the bread and wine. So we can define presence as a sacramental and spiritually reality.[63] The bread and wine are sacramentally and spiritually changed, so that those who, in faith, partake of them find the bread and wine to be the body and blood of Christ.[64] They are changed so that an encounter between God and us can occur. We are united with God. In this way, the body and blood of Christ are gifts from God.

We are called to receive the body and blood of Christ with faith and thanksgiving. In Communion, Christ gives himself in the elements and we feed on them in our hearts by faith with thanksgiving. The elements are offerings from God to the believer, who is waiting to receive them. When this offering is met by faith, "a life-giving encounter results"[65] where Christ is present with the believer and a personal relationship between Christ and the believer commences.

Communion is at once both the "most personal" and the "most corporate" or public of acts.[66] The congregation works together so everyone can receive the elements. People come forward, standing in line or kneeling together at an altar rail in groups. Each person receives the bread and wine individually. From the minister's vantage point, the congregation moves in sequence toward the altar while others sing and pray. Then in sacramental, spiritual moments, each believer receives the elements. While people are moving and singing, others have solitary moments of personal relationship with God.

The theological themes I have explained briefly can be studied for a lifetime. Throughout the centuries of Christian history, many theologians have added to our understanding of the mystery that is Communion. The material I've presented here is on a spectrum of belief. On one end is the belief that Communion memorializes the Lord's Supper, and on the other end Communion makes Christ present in body and blood. Because of my own experience and witness, I am closer to the belief that Christ is really present in this sacred meal.

When speaking to our children about this sacred meal, we should offer theological themes to enhance their worship experience and their understanding of their relationship with God. At first their understanding will be simplistic, but over time, seasoned by each experience, they will deepen their understanding.

Activity Two

With which theological theme do you identify most? Why? How might you explain Communion to your child?

CHAPTER 6 ❧

Growing a Soul

You don't have a soul. You are a Soul. You have a body.
(C.S. Lewis)[67]

Invariably when I speak with parents of young children, our conversations will turn toward teenagers. Knowing I have more than a decade of experience in youth ministry and two teenagers of my own, parents will prod me with questions about teenagers going to church, teenage rebellion, and teenagers' faith. At a dinner for more than thirty parents of eighth graders, a parent asked, "So how do we keep this all going?" He was referring to his daughter's spiritual development. Noticing every parent in the room was listening attentively, eagerly awaiting my answer, I swallowed hard, knowing what I was about to tell them. I said, "The most important factor to keeping your child involved in church and faith and spirituality is you." It was not the elixir they wanted to hear, but the truth is not always pleasant.

We are key to our children's and teenagers' development. Christian Smith, author of *Soul Searching: the Religious and*

Spiritual Lives of American Teenagers, says parents have far more influence on children than they realize. He writes, "For better or worse, most parents in fact still do profoundly influence their adolescents—often more than do their peers—their children's apparent resistance and lack of appreciation not withstanding."[68] He adds that what is most important to future religious, spiritual habits, activities in adulthood are "significant social relationships." At the top of the list of significant relationships, Smith's research places parents. So you as parents have immense influence on growing the soul of your child. More than any youth minister or Sunday school teacher or friend, you are key to making sure your child has a deep, well-formed spiritual well.

Not long ago, St. Matthew's Church, which is located in Bedford, New York, celebrated its two-hundredth anNIversary. As a part of the celebration, the church chose to rededicate the one-hundred-year-old Bedford Cross. It is an immense, gray stone, Celtic cross standing some thirty feet high. Carved on the base are the words *Pax et Bonum*, which means peace and goodwill. The cross is adjacent to the church, across a state road on a triangular piece of land. It was originally erected so travelers passing by it would be able to say a prayer. It stands in an open field of grass with majestic maple trees lining the edges of the roads.

The cross stands on the site of the First Particular Baptist Church, where people worshiped in the nineteenth century. When the church closed, the land was sold to St. Matthew's and the church building was removed. Near the church was a well used to provide water for the horses while people worshiped. When the church was closed, the well was filled in—and, until recently, forgotten.

As the workers were preparing the area around the cross for the rededication, and planting several new maple trees along one edge of the triangle, one of the workers suddenly fell into the well. Not to worry; he only sunk to his waist. More surprised than anything, he scrambled out. Over the years, the dirt used to fill in the well had settled, creating an empty pocket near the surface. But this was not noticeable because the grass held the topsoil in place, so there was no evidence of the well or the treacherous gap.

This hidden well is like some people's spiritual wells. A covered-over spiritual well results from abstaining from any spiritual activity. Being too busy to pray, too exhausted to go to church, too distracted to read the Bible, or never coming together as a family to read a devotion or discuss a spiritual concern—all of these cause our wells to cover over. Neglect is the reason spiritual wells become covered. And when they are covered, we lose contact with God and our ability to make good, faithful decisions.

Spiritual wells can become bug-infested pools of sin, too. Sin is those actions that distort our relationship with God and our neighbor. It is those activities that stand in opposition to loving God and loving our neighbor. When we become jealous of our neighbors, resentful of our parents, or the centers of our own lives, we are sinful. This sinfulness leads us to make poor decisions and take on abusive habits. We ignore God. We ignore our family and friends. We become self-centered and egocentric. We are caught up in making our lives images of materialistic perfection. We own all the right things and proudly show them off to our families, friends, and neighbors. Because of this bug infestation in our spiritual wells, we are never happy or satisfied.

Spiritual wells can be ignored in an additional way. A well can run dry. This happens when our lives are too stressful. Unlike neglect or sin, stress simply depletes all of the life-giving water in the well. It is not that we forget to pray, read the Bible, or go to church. No, we do all of those and more. On my refrigerator there is a magnet that says, "Lord grant me patience, but hurry!" This typifies the stress that leads to an empty well. This stress leads to sleepless nights filled with prayers like, "God, please let me have a couple of hours of sleep." Our minds are stressed and need a place to process and let go of life's difficulties. If we don't give the space to allow such mental processing to occur, our minds simply stay active when our bodies are exhausted. Prayer, worship, and Bible reading become activities that we use to blot out the stress. Instead of filling us, spiritual activities are simply more chores to rush through.

A good well requires attention. It requires care. It requires thoughtfulness. We know one when we see it. The stonework around the well is in good condition. The stones rise several feet off the ground to keep dirt and dust from defiling the water. There may even be a cover to keep out snakes and bugs. And when we look down the well, the water is dark and clear. We feel the water's coolness rising up from the well and it smells refreshing and clean. As we pull the bucket of water from the well and taste the water, it is good. The life-giving water restores us with vigor and purpose. It cleans our bodies and minds. The spiritual well operates much like an actual well.

A well-tended spiritual well indicates spiritual maturity. Frances Vaughan, Ph.D., writes in *What Is Spiritual Intelligence?* that spiritual maturity is "expressed through wisdom and compassionate action in the world."[69] She adds, "Spiritual intelligence is necessary for discernment in making spiritual choices that contribute to psychological well-being and overall healthy human development." For parents, our goal is to develop our children's SQ so they gain wisdom to make good choices and develop a care for others and the world around them. Central to that wisdom and care is acknowledgment of God.

What are the signs of wisdom and care? Research by the National Study of Youth and Religion, led by Christian Smith, clearly shows the signs of spiritual maturity. This study found that teens who are devoted to church (i.e. attend church weekly, faith is very or extremely important in everyday life, feel very or extremely close to God, involved in a youth group, pray a few times a week or more, and read scripture once or twice a month or more) are much more likely to avoid risk behaviors. The same holds true for those teens who are regular attendees (i.e. attend church two or three times a month or weekly, faith ranges from very to not very important in everyday life; closeness to God, youth group involvement, prayer, and scripture reading varied). Both groups were less likely to get into trouble than other groups of teens. The study said "devoted" and "regular" teens are less likely to smoke cigarettes, more likely not to drink alcohol, more likely not to smoke marijuana, less likely to cut class, and more likely to get better grades. Parents of these teens reported their teens were less likely to be rebellious.[70]

The study found more positive results about teens who are "devoted" or "regular." In terms of their emotional well-being, these teens typically have better body image, are less likely to feel depressed, are less likely to feel alone or misunderstood, are less likely to feel invisible, are more likely to feel cared for, are more likely to have plans for the future, and are more likely to think about the meaning of life. Moreover, these teens are more likely to have given more than twenty dollars of their own money to an organization or cause, to do volunteer service and to do it more often, to care for the needs of the poor, to care about the elderly, and to care about equality between different racial groups.[71]

In short, teens who find church and faith important make better decisions, feel better about themselves, and care more about others. Following the definition of spiritual maturity, we see that those teens who regularly practice the habits that develop SQ obtain spiritual maturity. They have the wisdom to avoid risk behaviors and act compassionately in the world.

Many teens live their lives this way:

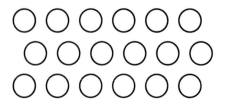

Each circle represents an activity such as school, work, homework, talking on the phone, instant messaging, hanging out with friends, talking with their parents, going to practice, sleeping, watching television, going on a date, partying, playing in a game, attending church, going to a youth group event, extracurricular activities, and on and on. On any given weekend, teens have many activities from which to choose. For most teens, attending church or a church youth group is just one more from which to pick; it's a buffet of choices. Each circle is as important as any other. So whatever they are in the mood to do or are required to do, by school or parents, they will do.

The goal of SQ is to move away from the buffet, where every activity is as good as the next, to spiritual maturity. It is to grow a soul. The mature soul orients your child to look this way:

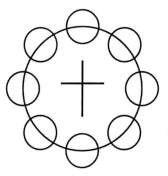

When a child develops his or her soul to spiritual maturity by using the religious and spiritual habits defined earlier, they are no longer tossed about by their emotions and are less influenced by outside sources, especially those leading to risk behaviors. They have an identity. That identity is found in their soul. It is exhibited by their behavior. They make good decisions. They make the right choices. Moreover, they care about others. They care about those in need. They have what Loehr and Schwartz call a "connection to a deeply held set of values and to a purpose beyond our self-interest."[72] They have developed the top of their pyramid. They have developed an SQ that rests atop of Loehr and Schwartz's pyramid of the four dynamic energies or intelligences.

SQ development that leads to spiritual maturity is a gift we give to our children. It's not simply that our children make good decisions, but they have meaning in their lives. Loehr and Schwartz call living life with meaning as being "full engagement." To live a life fully engaged is when "we care deeply, when we feel that what we are doing really matters."[73] As parents, to help our children live fully engaged lives is a gift. Our highest goal should be to help our children develop their souls so they may live good and meaningful lives.

My prayer for you is this: I pray that you and your child develop small, daily rituals of prayer, Bible reading, and devotions. May you find a church where you can regularly attend worship services. May you help your child trowel and spoon a deep spiritual well that is filled with the divine elixir of love, grace, and mercy. And I pray that you may watch your child grow into an adult who makes good decisions, cares about others, and finds meaning in all aspects of his or her life.

Part Two

Forty Days of Devotions

Devotionals, or meditations as they are also known, are important. They allow us to consider a line or two from the Scriptures, and in thinking about what has been said and the commentary that follows we are changed. Each devotional is meant to shovel more soil from the bottoms of our spiritual wells so they deepen more and more.

There are forty devotionals in this section. If you choose, you may read one with your family each day. You may also choose to read the devotionals as a part of your family's Lenten discipline. Lent is a church season that includes the forty days from Ash Wednesday to Holy Saturday, excluding Sundays. For centuries, Christians have used this time as a means to prepare for the celebration of Easter. Today, some people give up something that is a symbolic temptation, like chocolate. Other people add a special activity like Bible reading or devotionals. So the following devotionals may be your family's Lenten practice. Or you could use them any time and in any order, by picking a topic.

You will notice that after each commentary there are two levels of questions. Level I questions are simpler and are meant for younger children. Level II are more complex and abstract questions and are meant for school-age children. Choose the questions that are most engaging for your family.

DAY ONE: ASH WEDNESDAY

The Beginning

> Jesus ... was led by the Spirit in the desert, where he stayed for forty days.
>
> (Luke 4:1-2a NIV)

Forty days is a long time—almost a month and a half. Think about how hard it must have been for Jesus to be away from his family and friends for such a long time. So why did he go? Why not stay home by the warm fire with those he loved and cared for? Jesus went to the desert to become spiritually stronger. He took that time to become completely and totally focused on his goals and mission. In the desert, Jesus had no distractions. He focused only on God's goals for him and the mission God had for him. This forty-day set of devotions is a way for us to grow closer to God, become better and stronger, and focus on God's goals for us and his mission for us, too.

Level I

How many weeks are in forty days?

What can you give up for forty days so you can be more like Jesus?

What can you do for forty days so you can be a better and stronger person?

Level II

Who in the Bible spent forty days alone with God? Look it up. (Ex. 34:28; Deut. 9:9)

What might be some things in your life that distract you from thinking about God or what he does?

Day Two

Temptation

> The Devil, playing on his hunger, gave the first test: "Since you're God's Son, command this stone to turn into a loaf of bread."
>
> (Luke 4:3 TMB)

Jesus was all alone in the desert for many days and was very hungry. I imagine he was hoping to be closer to God in the desert. I wonder if he wanted to hear again the voice that said to him at his baptism, "You are my Son, chosen and marked by my love, pride of my life." But he didn't. Something else happened. Someone visited him. Who? The Devil, that's who. What did the Devil want from Jesus? The Devil wanted Jesus to do a magic trick: turn stone into bread. But Jesus remembered his goal. He remembered he was to obey God. Jesus wouldn't obey the Devil. He obeyed only God.

Level I

How do you think Jesus felt while he was in the desert?
Did Jesus listen to the Devil?

Level II

What tempts you?
How might Jesus help you when you're tempted?

DAY THREE

Habits

> Worship the Lord your God and only the Lord your God.
> Serve him with absolute single-heartedness.
>
> (Luke 4:8 TMB)

The devil tested Jesus three times. Jesus' second answer was that we are to serve only God. Remembering Easter, we know serving God has a reward. We serve God, even in hard times, because we know and remember good times lie ahead for us. One way we serve God is to do something every day, like saying prayers or reading the Bible. If we do it every day, we make a new habit. Habits of devotion are important because they help us grow. So as you make a new habit, remember you will be rewarded by your efforts. By taking on a new devotional habit, you grow stronger and better. Most importantly, you grow closer to God.

Level I

What are some things you do every day that are good habits? How do they make you stronger or better?

Level II

Jesus quoted Deuteronomy 6:13. What is so important about the sixth chapter of Deuteronomy? Look it up.
The Shema is a prayer that Jews—even today—are instructed to learn and say daily. It can be found in Deuteronomy 6:4-9. Next time you visit a Jewish friend, you may see something affixed to the door jam of the front door. Ask your friend about it. Inside it is a copy of the Shema.
What does it mean to love God with strength?

DAY FOUR

Angels

He was with the wild beasts; and the angels ministered unto him.

(Mark 1:13 KJV)

Animals were certainly in the wilderness where Jesus was. Some of those animals probably were very dangerous, like scorpions and lions. The Bible doesn't say that Jesus is a super "Dr. Doolittle," one who makes friends with the animals. In ancient days, maybe more so than today, living and sleeping in the wild was dangerous because the animals might attack you. Fortunately for Jesus in that dangerous place, angels came to minister or take care of him. They protected him. Jesus hadn't eaten in many days so he was weak. The angels made sure Jesus was OK. God had not forgotten Jesus, even in the wilderness—he sent the angels to care for him. Angels work for God. God sent the angels to protect and care for him.

Level I

What do you think the wilderness was like?
Was it peaceful or scary?
How do you think Jesus felt?
Do you think he was happy to have angels with him? Why?

Level II

What do you think the angels did for Jesus?
How can you be like an angel to others?

DAY FIVE

Denying God

> How often I've longed to gather your children, gather your children like a hen, her brood safe under her wings. But you refused and turned away.
>
> (Luke 13:34 TMB)

God loves us and wants us to be with him. He wants to protect us. Have you ever been to a farm? Have you seen chicks running? They want to explore their world, but they also sense that the world is huge and scary. So the chicks dart out a little and then get scared and run back under their mother's wings. They feel safe under her wings. They know she will protect them no matter what. She will even die to protect them. But the mother cannot protect the chicks that stay away from her when danger comes. She calls out to them when danger is near, but the chicks must hear her and follow her warning. So when a fox or an owl is close by, only the chicks that listen and return to her are safe under her wings. It's this way with God—he is there to guide us, but we have to listen to him through the Holy Spirit.

Level I

What is a mother hen like?
What are chicks like?

Level II

What is a safe place for you?
How does God make you feel safe?

DAY SIX

Sacrifice

"Leave your country, your family, and your father's house for a land that I will show you."

(Gen. 12:1 TMB)

God spoke these words to Abram. When God calls us into action, we often have to give up things. Sometimes those things are small; other times they are great. Sometimes we are very willing to give up the things God asks of us; other times we are very unwilling. We don't know if this call from God was easy for Abram, but God certainly asks a lot from him. Abram has to give up everything he knows. He gives up his country where he lives. He gives up his family and his father's house where he felt safe and secure. He leaves his friends. He leaves everything that is familiar to him. He does all of this on a promise from God.

Level I

Have you gone on a trip and left your favorite stuffed animal, toy, or pet at home?
How did it feel?
How did it feel when you came home?

Level II

God speaks to us in many ways. God often speaks through prayer, sometimes through dreams, and in our quiet times. He also speaks to us through our friends and families. Most importantly, God speaks to us through the Bible. How can you become a better listener for God's voice?
What is God asking you to give up so you can follow him more?

DAY SEVEN

Jesus

> He went on teaching from town to village, village to town,
> but keeping on a steady course toward Jerusalem.
>
> (Luke 13:22 TMB)

Jesus was the greatest teacher of all time. The lessons he taught the world two thousand years ago are still important for us to learn today. Yet, Jesus was not just a great teacher. He also healed people who were sick. As he taught and healed, he moved from town to village, and each day he moved toward Jerusalem. He kept moving toward Palm Sunday, Good Friday, and, most importantly, Easter. God didn't send Jesus just to teach the world right from wrong, although he did. God didn't send him just to heal people. God sent Jesus to the world to save us from sin, the wrong things we do. So he taught and healed, and moved toward Jerusalem, where he would save us.

Level I

What do you like the most about your teachers?
Remember Jesus taught most often through parables. What is your favorite parable and why?

Level II

How do you live your daily life, but also keep a steady course toward God's purposes for us?
How can praying to God help you stay on a steady course?

DAY EIGHT

God's Shield

> "Don't be afraid, Abram, I am your shield; your reward shall
> be very great."
>
> (Gen. 15:2 NRSV)

Abram had been a faithful follower of God. He did all that God asked of him, but then God sensed doubt and fear in Abram's heart. How could this be? Abram left his family, friends, and livelihood. He suffered through famine, and faced enemies. He traveled constantly for many miles. Through it all, God protected him. God was his shield. Abram became wealthy with gold and herds of animals. But Abram wanted more. He wanted another sign, a son. Why? Simply, he was human and he needed God's support and encouragement to be sure he was on the right path. God is invisible but he gives us tangible signs; we must be watchful and attentive to see them. Maybe it's a verse in a Bible reading, or a plan that falls perfectly into place, or a kind word at just the right time from a friend or even a stranger—God's signs are all around us.

Level I

What does God's shield look like? Draw a picture.
What does God's shield do?

Level II

What are some of God's tangible signs of his presence and help?
Has God given you a tangible sign?

DAY NINE

God's Gift

> This is how much God loved the world; He gave his Son, his one and only Son.
>
> (John 3:16 NRSV)

These familiar words echo far and wide. So much has been said about these words and yet so much more can and will be said about them. Jesus is a gift to us. What does that mean? God gave us Jesus not because we earned it. If we had, then it wouldn't have been a gift. God gave us Jesus not because we expected it. If we had, then it would have been a bribe. God gave us Jesus because he loves us. There was risk for God in giving us this gift. What if we didn't like it? What if we didn't care for it? What if we just threw it out? What if no one cared for Jesus anymore? It could have happened, and it still could.

Level I

What has been your favorite gift? Why?
Who gave it to you?

Level II

Why did God give us Jesus?
What would happen if no one cared about Jesus anymore?

DAY TEN

Rejection

> Then he began to teach them that the Son of Man (Jesus) must undergo great suffering, and be rejected.
>
> (Mark 8:31 NRSV)

Have you ever been rejected? Jesus was. Not only that, but he knew it was coming. Most of us have felt rejection of some kind, especially when we were young. Maybe it was a brother who told us, "Go away! Stop bothering me!" Or maybe when we walked down the hall at school, we saw someone pointing and laughing at us, or we overheard our name being said, followed by more laughing. Rejection is tough. But what did Jesus do when so many people, even his friends, rejected him? Jesus stood firm. He didn't hide. He knew what God expected of him and he did it. Thank God, he did! Even though Jesus was rejected, he obeyed God, and in doing so, saved us all.

Level I

How does it feel when someone says to you, "Go away!"?
Have you ever been afraid of walking down the hallway at school or riding the bus because you thought someone would make fun of you?

Level II

When rejection happens to you, how can you stand firm like Jesus?
If a friend of yours is rejected, how can you help him or her?

DAY ELEVEN

Patience

> For three years now I've come to this tree expecting apples
> and not one apple have I found. Chop it down!
>
> (Luke 13:7 TMB)

If my television or computer didn't work for three weeks or even three days, I would be tempted to throw it out. It's hard to wait. In fact, the root word for *patience* means "to suffer." So to wait for something is to suffer. In our suffering, we can turn to God for help. What you gave up or added on for forty days is not just to make you a better person. Maybe you gave up food because deep down inside you knew times like Lent are good excuses for losing weight. Or you thought by not watching so much television you'd have more time to be with your family. Maybe you have always wanted to read the Bible more, so you have decided to read it. These are good things, but by now you might be beginning to see that a new habit is hard to keep. So what to do? Turn to God. The true purpose of Lent is to cause us to turn to God for help. So ask God to help you stay committed to your new habit.

Level I

What is your favorite kind of apple?
If you went to the apple orchard in the springtime, would you see apples? Why or why not?
If you didn't see apples on the tree would you cut it down?

Level II

What has been the hardest part of keeping your new habit in the last week? What helped you?
Did you pray to God for help? Why? Why not?

DAY TWELVE

Even Jesus Got Tired

> Jacob's well was still there. Jesus, worn out by the trip, sat down at the well.
>
> (John 4:6 TMB)

Jesus did many things in his life. He prayed to God often. He healed many people. He taught crowds of people to follow God. He even walked on water. So how is it that Jesus got tired? Jesus couldn't be tired, because he was "Jesus," right? Wrong! Often we think of Jesus as some kind of comic book superhero, but he was not. Nor was Jesus a magician. The power he has comes from God. Still, Jesus was also just as human as you and I. He needed to sleep. He needed to eat. He even became tired from traveling.

Level I

How do you feel after a long trip in the car?
How do you feel when you haven't eaten in a long time?

Level II

What does Jesus do when he gets tired?
Does he give up on his journey because it is long and hard?
When you get tired of working on your new habit, what can you do to stay focused on God's goals and mission for you?

DAY THIRTEEN

God Provides

> Take the staff you used to strike the Nile. And go. I'm going to be present before you there on the rock at Horeb. You are to strike the rock. Water will gush out of it and the people will drink.
>
> (Ex. 17:6 TMB)

The Israelites had been walking in the wilderness without a drop of water to drink. They were thirsty and tired. They complained and threatened Moses. They said, "We need water." Who could blame them? Human beings can live for about forty days without food, but only for a few days without water. So Moses turned to God for help. And God provided the Israelites what they needed. It was not magic Moses used. No, he walked ahead of the people, found the place where God was, and struck a rock. The water flowed, perhaps from a spring hidden just underneath the rock. It was God's power Moses used to find the water, not magic.

Level I

Have you ever seen a stream bubbling up from underneath the ground or seen water bubbling up from underneath the water in a lake? If you have, was the water hot or cold? Did you notice all of the plant life around the stream? What did it look like?

Level II

Thinking about the rain, sun, and fertile soil, how does God provide for his creation?
What and how does God provide in your life?
What do you ask God to provide for you?

DAY FOURTEEN

Strength in the Lord

> He satisfies you with good things, and your youth is renewed like an eagle's.
>
> (Ps. 103:5 NRSV)

Have you ever felt like you could run forever or work all day without stopping? When we feel God's glory, we have power to do anything. Imagine that after forty days of Lent you wake up fresh and ready to take on the world. It is right for you to feel this way because you have worked hard all during Lent. Now, you have formed yourself anew. You have proven to yourself that with God's help you can accomplish more than you thought you could. You feel like running. No, you feel like you can fly like an eagle and soar in the clouds.

Level I

What would it be like to be an eagle?
What would you see? Where would you go?

Level II

Imagine yourself after forty days of working on your new habit.
Will you feel like a slug or an eagle? Why?
If not an eagle, about what can you pray to God to help you be an eagle and not a slug after forty days?

DAY FIFTEEN

God's Presence

> The angel of God appeared to him in flames of fire blazing out
> of the middle of a bush. He looked. The bush was blazing but
> it didn't burn up. And Moses said, "What' going on here?"
> (Ex. 3:3 TMB)

Moses saw a bush burning in front of him, but the bush didn't burn up. Naturally, he asked, "Why?" He was curious and amazed, but he was also confused and filled with disbelief. We need to remember that Moses moved closer to the bush, but he could have run away screaming in fear of it. He had a choice. God wants all of us to be closer to him. Yet he does not force us to do so. So he gives us signs of his presence, maybe not as direct as a burning bush, though many people can point to "burning bush" moments in their lives. These signs are times when we can choose to be closer to God or not. These signs can be found in doing good deeds for others or praying. Signs from God are all around us.

Level I

Have you ever watched a fire burning in a fireplace or a campfire?
What happened? How did it feel?
What do you think Moses felt?

Level II

What signs has God given you?
How did those signs make you feel? Why? (If you have never seen signs of God's presence, ask him to show you some!)

DAY SIXTEEN

Holy Ground

> Remove the sandals from your feet, for the place on which you are standing is holy ground.
>
> (Ex. 3:5 NRSV)

Moses approached the burning bush. Maybe he wanted to warm himself. Then God told him to stop and remove his shoes because the place was holy. What does this mean? Wasn't Moses in the middle of the desert? What made this place more special than any other? Well, for one, God made the place special. Does God make other places special, too? Yes! We know this when we come to a place and stop to admire its beauty. We are drawn to the beauty of a majestic waterfall. We are drawn to the beauty of the setting sun. We are drawn to the wideness of a green valley or the heights of a mountain. All of these are examples of holy ground. Archbishop Desmond Tutu of South Africa, in witnessing the forgiveness occurring between whites and blacks there, said people should take off their shoes because they were standing on holy ground. Anywhere we see the overt power of God in creation or in our lives, especially in forgiveness, there is holy ground.

Level I

What is it like to forgive someone?
Is it hard? How does it make you feel?

Level II

What is holy ground in your life? Where do you find it?

DAY SEVENTEEN

Selfishness

> He signed on with a citizen there who assigned him to his fields to slop the pigs.
>
> (Luke 15:15 TMB)

On a farm near our house, there is a pig named Charlotte who is only six months old. When I first met her she was the size of an ordinary housecat, but now she weighs nearly 250 pounds! She's huge. If I hadn't seen her when she was very young, I'd never have believed she was only six months old and had been so small. The funny thing about pigs is we say they are stupid when actually they're pretty smart. What makes us think they are stupid? Maybe it is because they carry their heads low to the ground. It's really hard for them to look up. Also, they always are covered in dirt. Yet, Charlotte knows her name better than my cat. I think what makes us think pigs are stupid is they are only concerned about food, and they don't seem to care about what they eat or where they lie. Yuck! So we think of pigs as selfish and uncaring about themselves. Charlotte seems to have little concern for others, unless of course they are bringing her food. She doesn't take care of herself. At least my cat can play and groom herself!

Level I

Have you ever acted selfishly? How did you feel when you did? And why?

Level II

How does God want us to treat our bodies and souls? What is an example?

DAY EIGHTEEN

Bullying

> Each morning and evening for forty days, Goliath took his
> stand and made his speech.
>
> (Ex. 17:16 TMB)

Two armies, the Israelites and the Philistines, sat on opposing
hills. A valley lay between them. Each day for forty days, a huge
Philistine soldier, ten feet tall and stronger than any man in either
army, walked out into the valley and taunted and bullied the
Israelite army. He dared the Israelites to send one of their soldiers
to fight him. He said if the Israelite won, then the Philistine
people would become their slaves and serve the Israelites. If the
Philistine won, then the Israelite people would become their
slaves and serve the Philistines. For forty days, no one from the
Israelites dared to step out and challenge the Philistines.

Level I

Who are bullies?
Have you ever been bullied, or have you been a bully?

Level II

Does God sometimes call us to fight others?
If so, how and when? If not, why?

DAY NINETEEN

Godly Living

And Jesus said, "It's who you are and the way you live that count before God."

(John 4:23 TMB)

Jesus clearly says what is important to God. And deep within all of us, we know what it is. Jesus teaches us that God cares about what makes us who we are, what we care about, and how we treat others. For example, God doesn't care how much money someone has. If he or she has money, fine. It is how we use our money that concerns God. Jesus teaches that God cares about what is inside us. It is what we think about other people that is important. Do we gossip or tell bad stories about other people? Do we ignore people because of the way they look or how they act? Do we make fun of other people and hurt them with our words? Or do we help those who are hurting? Do we stand up to those who say bad things about other people? God wants us to be caring, brave, loving, and kind. Jesus says how we live our life matters to God.

Level I

Have you ever seen someone laugh at or make fun of another person?
Have you ever been made fun of, or made fun of another person?

Level II

What does it take to stand up against gossip?
What does it take to defend the weak?
Have you ever done so? If so, why? If not, why not?

DAY TWENTY

Fairness

> "Your brother has come, and your father has killed the fatted calf, because he has got him back safe and sound." Then he became angry and refused to go in.
>
> (Luke 15:27-28a NRSV)

His younger brother had returned. When he left, in the first place, he did so with lots of money. And he stuck his older brother with more work and responsibilities. The younger brother went off and played. He spent all of his money, while his older brother stayed home and worked. Now that the younger brother had returned, the older brother thought, *Well, that figures. He comes home after blowing all that money and now Dad throws him a big party! This is so unfair! What about all the hard work I did? Doesn't that mean more?* I cannot think of a brother or sister who wouldn't be upset in this situation.

Level I

Do you think your parents always treat you fairly?
Is the older brother right to be upset? Why?

Level II

Think about the father's position. Why would he throw a party for the son who returns?
How is God like the father? How are you like the son who returns?

DAY TWENTY-ONE

Signs

> When your children ask their parents in time to come, "What do these stones mean?" then you shall let your children know, "Israel crossed over the Jordan here on dry ground."
>
> (Josh. 4:21b-22 NRSV)

The twelve tribes of Israel had traveled in the wilderness for forty years. Now God had dried up the Jordan River, just like he had done for them at the Red Sea. All the twelve tribes, each with thousands of people, crossed the Jordan on dry ground. Joshua, their new leader, told them to place twelve stones together to be a sign and a memorial so that they and their children would remember their forty years in the wilderness. Today, we have signs all around us. There are street signs, signs for the bathroom, and even signs at school. There are also many signs at church. Lent is a sign and a memorial. During Lent, we remember that Jesus spent forty days in the wilderness. We give up things to remember how Jesus gave up food during his wilderness time. We also give up things so we don't forget all that God has given us.

Level I

Name some signs you have seen today. What were they for? Name some signs you see at church. What are they for?

Level II

Name a Christian sign or symbol that is important to you. Why is it important to you?

Day Twenty-Two

God Is the Best!

Let's march into his presence singing praises, lifting the rafters with our hymns! And why? Because God is the best.

(Ps. 95:2-3a TMB)

God is the best! Nothing is better than God. Why? First, God made everything. Sometimes that is hard to believe. Everything, really? Maybe it's better to think of it this way: Without God, nothing would exist. God started creation and God watches over everything, seeing that creation continues. Therefore, because God started creation, he owns it. It's his. And we are his. Second, God loves his creation. He loves the mountains and the valleys, the tallest tree and the tiniest plant. He loves the elephant and the mouse. God loves it all. God also loves human beings—he loves them a lot. God doesn't love only special human beings or the most perfect among us. Instead, he loves all human beings. That means he loves you, too! Indeed, God is the best!

Level I

Name a reason why God is the best.

Level II

Since God created everything, how do we treat his creation?
How do we treat ourselves?
How do we treat others?

DAY TWENTY-THREE

Jesus Is Sad

Now Jesus wept.

(John 11:35 TMB)

Jesus' friend Lazarus had died. Jesus was away when he died. Four days after Lazarus's death, Jesus went to Bethany, where Lazarus's body had been placed in a tomb. Jesus went there because he wanted to raise Lazarus from the dead. Lazarus's sister Mary came to him crying and upset that Jesus was not there when Lazarus was dying. Mary said to Jesus that if he had been there Lazarus would not have died. He would have healed Lazarus and made him better. Seeing how upset Mary and the others were at Lazarus' death, Jesus was upset, too. Jesus cried. Sometimes it is hard to think that the Son of God, the Messiah, would cry. We have all heard, "Men don't cry." But here was Jesus crying over the death of his friend, Lazarus. If it is OK for Jesus to cry, then it is okay for us to cry also.

Level I

Why do you cry?
How does it make you feel?

Level II

Why is it important for us to see that Jesus cried?
Name some of the other emotions Jesus felt.

DAY TWENTY-FOUR

Miracles

> There's a little boy here who has five barley loaves and two fish.
>
> (John 4:9 TMB)

A huge crowd followed Jesus. They wanted to see and hear the famous Jesus speak and see him miraculously heal the sick. Jesus saw the large crowd, and being a good host told his disciples that they needed to feed those people. His disciples were flabbergasted. They said, "Jesus, the crowd is huge. We don't have that much money!" So, they searched for food. The only food they could find was from a little boy who had brought five loaves of bread and two fish. Jesus smiled. He gave thanks to God for the bread and fish, which is like us saying grace before a meal. Then, he fed five thousand people with just five loaves of bread and two fish. What a miracle! And all because a little boy gave his bread and fish to Jesus. Jesus showed us that the little boy's gift was just as important as any other gift brought by an adult. All of us, no matter what our age, are important to God, and we all have something that makes the world a better place.

Level I

What can you do to make the world a better place?

Level II

What is a miracle?
Have you ever seen one in your life, or heard about one in the life of another?

DAY TWENTY-FIVE

Freedom

> You can readily recall, can't you, how at one time the more you did just what you felt like doing—not caring about others, not caring about God—the worse your life became and the less freedom you had?
>
> (Romans 6:19a TMB)

One day when I was a boy I rode my bike up Long Ridge Road to the small market in the woods. The ride was about three miles of fairly flat pavement along a double-yellow-lined road. The shoulder on the road was narrow and cars sped by quickly. Sometimes, big trucks whooshed by. It was dangerous, but the road was easier to ride on than Hunting Ridge Road, which was very hilly, but much safer. My parents allowed me only to ride on that safe road. It wasn't enough for me that I could ride my bike to the market. I had to be able to ride my bike on the road I wanted to ride on. So I chose to ride on the flatter, more dangerous road, and I got caught. My mom saw me riding. When I got home, I was grounded. I was not able to ride my bike anywhere, because I hadn't obeyed my parents. When I was riding on the dangerous road, I hadn't cared how that might have made my parents feel. I only wanted a flatter ride, even if it was dangerous.

Level I

Name a time when you were given a time-out or grounding. How did that make you feel?

Level II

Because Jesus died for our sins and brought us back to God, does that mean we can live any way we want? Why?

DAY TWENTY-SIX

Mistakes

That stone the masons threw out—it's now the cornerstone!

(Luke 20:18 TMB)

Have you ever rejected something or someone and then later realized you were wrong, that you made a mistake? I know I have. I don't like to make mistakes, but when I do, I try to learn from them. Sometimes we learn best from mistakes. When we reject someone or something and are wrong, what do we do? Sometimes we try to deny that we did anything wrong, but that's lying, and lying only makes the wrong worse. Sometimes we hide or avoid the person we hurt, but that makes it worse, too. Then the mistake stands between us and the person we hurt. The best thing to do when we make a mistake or wrong someone is to say we did it and apologize or ask for forgiveness. That is what God wants from us when we make a mistake. When we ask for forgiveness, God always gives us a second chance. Often it is easier for us to see we have hurt another person than it is to see we have hurt God. But when we pray to God for forgiveness of our wrongs, we realize we have made mistakes that hurt God. We ask God for forgiveness and he does.

Level I

Name a mistake you recently made.
What did you do when you made the mistake?
Have you ever rejected someone? How did it feel?

Level II

How do you feel after you have apologized to someone for your mistake?
How do you feel after you pray to God for forgiveness?

DAY TWENTY-SEVEN

Watchfulness

> Be alert, be present. I'm about to do something brand-new.
> It's bursting out! Don't you see it?
>
> (Isaiah 43:19 TMB)

Spring is close. Don't you see it? What does it mean to be alert? What does it mean to be present? Well, it means we are aware of what is happening all around us. It means being watchful for signs. They can be hard to see if we are not aware. Signs of spring are everywhere, but we must be watchful for them. Snowdrops are blooming. Daffodils are pushing through the soil. Flies are hatching in the river. The grass is turning green. Something brand new is happening. Spring is about to burst out. So what does it take for us to see the signs? We must be alert and present. But how? Well, for one, it takes our being less concerned about ourselves. When we feel comfortable about who we are, then we can be alert. When we know ourselves, we are less worried about what others think of us. Then we can be more alert and present to the wonders of God's creation bursting out.

Level I

Have you noticed any plants, animals, or bugs that are out for the first time this spring?
What are they and where did you see them?

Level II

What is brand new in you and waiting to burst out?
What are the signs of change in you?
What do you see God doing new in those around you?

DAY TWENTY-EIGHT

Jesus Versus Us

Scrub away my guilt, soak out my sins in your laundry.

(Ps. 51:2 TMB)

It is time to look more closely at the difference between Jesus, and you and me. The Bible tells us Jesus lived with no sin. What does this mean? It means Jesus did nothing to offend God during his time on earth. He lived exactly how God wants us to live. But we don't always live the way God wants us to live. We try to do everything God wants us to do, but we forget to put God first all the time. We become attracted to other things. Have you wished Lent would end sooner so you could eat brownies or chocolate again? It's hard not to have these thoughts. That is how we fall short of Jesus and God. When we are proud of our actions, regret what we have done for God, or wish we hadn't, we fail God. And that is wrong, but God forgives us. He scrubs away our wrong doings. He makes us better again. Why? Because he loves us. And that is one of the most important lessons of Lent.

Level I

What did you give up, or what new habit have you started?
Have you thought it was too difficult, or one day forgot to do it?
What have you learned about yourself from that?

Level II

Regret, pride, forgetfulness: which one has given you trouble?
Have you been quick to ask for and receive God's forgiveness?

DAY TWENTY-NINE

Palm Branches

> Others cut branches from the trees and threw them down as a welcome mat.
>
> (Matt. 21:8 TMB)

Riding a young colt, Jesus entered into the city of Jerusalem with all of his disciples and followers cheering him. They laid their robes before him. Soon other people, citizens from Jerusalem, cut down branches—we think they were from palm trees. They laid these branches before Jesus as a welcome mat. I have handed out palm branches on Palm Sunday to children for many years now. And naturally, they play with them. Some who are very skilled fold their palm branches into crosses, while others just pull apart the palm. Often, we hold up our branches, waving them like we are celebrating Jesus' arrival. But have you ever seen anyone use a palm branch as a welcome mat at a front door? I haven't. We tend to cherish our branches instead of using them as a means of welcoming a stranger or friend to our home. In fact, it seems we do the opposite of what the citizens of Jerusalem did for Jesus.

Level I

What is the purpose of the welcome mat at the front door of your home?

Level II

What do the palm branches that you get at church on Palm Sunday mean to you?

What does the church do with the left over palm branches from Palm Sunday?

What are some ways to welcome Jesus into your home and your heart?

DAY THIRTY

The Tethered Colt

As soon as you enter, you'll find a colt tethered, one that has never yet been ridden. Untie it and bring it.

(Mark 11:2 TMB)

Horses are beautiful animals. Even young ones are strong and full of life. At first, most horses don't like to be ridden. They need lots of training, or "breaking in." Then someone can ride them more easily. Jesus sends two of his disciples into a nearby village to find a horse so he can ride it into Jerusalem. He tells them exactly where they will find it and that it has never been ridden. We are surprised Jesus describes to them exactly where and what kind of horse they will find. Indeed, this is remarkable, but what is equally remarkable is Jesus chooses to ride a horse that has never been ridden. What if the horse throws Jesus off? What if Jesus cannot get the horse to obey his commands? Jesus is not worried; he knows he can handle even a colt that has never been ridden.

Level I

What do you like about horses?
What makes you afraid of horses?

Level II

Which is more powerful to you: that Jesus told his disciples where to find the horse and what kind it was, or that he rode a horse that had never been ridden?
What do his actions tell us about who he is?

DAY THIRTY-ONE

Good from Bad

I'm the only God there is—the only God who does things right and knows how to help.

(Isa. 45:21 TMB)

There is an old saying that says to make lemonade out of lemons. Lemons are very tart and sour tasting, but lemonade is sweet and tart, which is delicious. I often see God working in my life and the lives of the people around me much the same way. God takes a bad thing and makes it into something good. This is not to say that God causes the bad things to happen. Bad things happen because they are a part of our lives here on earth. God knows how to help us when bad things happen and turn them toward good. The ultimate example of this is when Jesus died on the cross. Jesus' death was very bad, but then he rose from the dead, which was the best thing of all. Jesus died to save us from the bad things we do. Jesus took the punishment we deserved for our bad, sinful things. Because of that, many people have come to know God. God does make lemonade out of lemons!

Level I

Taste a lemon slice. How does it taste?
Taste some lemonade. What is the difference?

Level II

Where in your life has God made lemonade out of lemons?
Name a bad thing that has happened. Pray to God, asking him to find the good in it and how he can help you.

DAY THIRTY-TWO

Tulips and Jesus

Just watch my servant blossom! Exalted, tall, head and shoulders above the crowd!

(Isa. 52:13 TMB)

This is the time of year when the tall flowers like daffodils and tulips start to come out of the ground. Look around your garden, a park nearby, or along the road. You will see long, thin, green stems push up through the ground. Some of the daffodil stems will have bright yellow tips. They will be the ones that bloom into flowers. Or maybe your mom or dad has bought some tulips and brought them home. Notice how tall the stems are. Compared to snow drops and crocuses, which bloom at the very end of winter, these flowers are very tall. Spring has truly arrived when the daffodils and tulips blossom. In this verse of scripture, Isaiah writes, for the fourth time, about God's "suffering servant." We Christians read these "songs" or poems and think of Jesus. At his resurrection, Jesus blossomed greater than life and especially greater than death. Jesus is above all others. He is the leader that all of us follow.

Level I

What happens to daffodils and tulips from the time they push up through the ground until their flowers open?

Level II

In what ways does the emergence of the flower from the earth and its blossoming remind you of Jesus?

DAY THIRTY-THREE

Lying

> Even though he'd never hurt a soul or said one word that wasn't true.
>
> (Isa. 53:9 TMB)

Have you ever played the game called "Mafia"? It's great fun. Basically, it is a game where you have to figure out who in a large group of players is lying. The game moves quickly as the group of "citizens" tries to discover who among them are members of the "mafia." Each round, while all the citizens have their eyes closed, the mafia votes off people from the group. The citizens open their eyes to discover which citizen has been voted off. The goal for the citizens is to try to discover all of the mafia members before all of the citizens have been voted off. Unfortunately, sometimes the citizens vote off innocent citizens! It is very disheartening for those who have been voted off by the other citizens. Often, that person will sit dejected or even get up to find something to eat. But as soon as the game is over, he or she jumps back in, wanting revenge for being voted off! Jesus never hurt a soul and never said one word that wasn't true. Many places in the New Testament affirm Jesus' innocence. Still, he was "voted off." He was crucified, even though he always told the truth.

Level I

How do you feel when you tell a lie?
How do you think others feel when they are lied to?

Level II

How do you think Jesus felt when he was accused of lying?
What would you have done if you were Jesus?

DAY THIRTY-FOUR

Faithfulness

Thank God—he's so good. His love never quits!

(Ps. 118:29 TMB)

So we have reached the beginning of the end. Palm Sunday is tomorrow, and then Holy Week. It is fitting that at the beginning of the end, we give thanks and praise to God. Making a new habit or giving something up is hard work. Some of you may have done a better job at it than others. Some of you may reflect upon this Lent and want to take on something more challenging next year. The last week of Jesus' life, which we celebrate as Holy Week, is a good time to reflect upon the last thirty-four days. It is a right time to look deeply at the difference between God and us. But now is the time to give thanks and praise, because we have been able to keep our discipline this Lent by focusing on God and asking for His help. God is good and his love for us never quits.

Level I

When was it hard to keep your forty-day discipline?
In what ways is God good? How has He been good to you?

Level II

As we look in our rearview mirror, in what ways did God help you become better and stronger?
Where was God guiding you along during the past thirty-four days?

DAY THIRTY-FIVE

The Jar of Alabaster

As he sat at the table, a woman came up with an alabaster jar of very costly ointment of nard, and she broke open the jar, she poured the ointment on his head.

(Mark 14:3 NRSV)

I heard recently that some people spend five hundred dollars for a haircut in New York City. Wow! But in comparison, the ointment put on Jesus' head cost much more. In fact, today in America, it would be worth around five thousand dollars. The jar alone was worth more than three hundred denarii. One denarius was equivalent to a day's pay to a common laborer in the Roman Empire. So this jar of oil was a very expensive luxury. The ointment was imported from the Himalayan Mountains, which are in the country of Nepal near China and India. Those mountains are thousands of miles away from the town of Bethany, in Israel. So the jar traveled by caravan or ship, or both, for thousands of miles. Why does the woman pour the oil on Jesus' head? The Bible tells us prophets poured the oil on the heads of kings in order to recognize their kingship. But Jesus tells his disciples that she pours the oil on his head because she is preparing his body for burial. The woman shows her love for Jesus, and she shows a deep respect for Jesus, the Son of God, by giving something very valuable to her friend Jesus, who was much more valuable to her.

Level I

Make a list of all the things you could buy for five thousand dollars. To whom would you give five thousand dollars? Why?

Level II

How can you develop a deep respect for Jesus in your life? What valuable things can you give Jesus? (It's probably something you can't see.)

DAY THIRTY-SIX

Satan Returns

> After Judas received the piece of bread, Satan entered him. Jesus said to him, "Do quickly what you are going to do."
>
> (John 13:27 NRSV)

We have come full circle. Satan is back. The last time Satan was on the scene was when Jesus was in the wilderness facing Satan's three temptations. Jesus withstood Satan's temptations and Satan withdrew. Now, Satan is back, but things seem different. The devil is not the one who is in control here. Jesus is. Satan enters Judas only after Jesus gives Judas the piece of bread. Jesus is the one who is in control. Yet Jesus also says to Judas/Satan that he is to act quickly, meaning the betrayal of Jesus. Here, we see a transition. The world is undergoing a radical change that ends with Jesus as ruler of the world and Satan defeated. When Jesus dies on the cross, he defeats sin, death, and Satan. But it is only Holy Tuesday, and Satan still has work to do.

Level I

Do you think Satan is real?
How is Jesus stronger than Satan?

Level II

Satan means adversary, the constant enemy of God and man, a supernatural evil being; in a more positive sense, he is permitted to be God's agent to present moral choices to humans.
Which part of the definition means more to you and why?

DAY THIRTY-SEVEN: HOLY WEDNESDAY

Betrayal

> Then one of the twelve, who was called Judas Iscariot, went to the chief priests and said, "What will you give me if I betray Jesus to you?" They paid him thirty pieces of silver.
>
> (Matt. 26:14-15 NRSV)

What is it to betray someone? First, betrayal can only happen between two people who are close. Strangers don't betray, because there has to be trust between the two people. Judas was the disciple who held the purse for the others; he was entrusted with the money. So Jesus and all the other disciples trusted Judas. Why then does Judas betray that trust? We don't know. The gospel writers don't give us a motive for Judas's actions. But it is safe to say his actions rose out of strong emotions. Also, we remember that Satan played a role in Judas's actions. He either pushed Judas further and further, or presented him with a moral dilemma, which led Judas to choose betrayal. We often shun Judas. We don't want to admit that it was a human being, just like you and me, who betrayed Jesus. Yet, in Holy Week we must look at the best and worst inside of us. We do so because we need to see just how great Jesus is compared to you and me.

Level I

Have you ever been hurt by a friend? If so, when, and what did it feel like?

Level II

What have you done to a friend that you regret?
What mistakes have you made in your relationship with God?
Are there ways you can betray Jesus or God?

Holy Wednesday Activity

This is a familiar activity for high school students in youth groups. Have everyone in your family write on a piece of paper the worst thing he or she has done. Don't show it to anyone or read it aloud. Fold the paper several times. Then go outside or to your fireplace and burn all the papers completely. Say this prayer or another one: "Lord, thank you for the life of your blessed Son, Jesus, who died on the cross for all of our sins. As these papers burn, free us from our sins both small and great. Draw us closer to you in love and peace. By your Holy Spirit make us whole. We ask all of this in the name of Jesus Christ, our Lord. Amen.[75]"

DAY THIRTY-EIGHT: MAUNDY THURSDAY

Fellowship

"I have eagerly desired to eat this Passover with you before I suffer."

(Luke 22:15a NRSV)

Jesus eagerly desired to eat with his closest friends, his disciples. With these words, Jesus showed us the love he had for his friends. He also showed us that fellowship is very important. What is fellowship? Pastor Rick Warren says fellowship is "experiencing life together."[76] When we look at the Gospels, we see that, for Jesus and his disciples, fellowship was experiencing the highs and lows of their lives together. The disciples traveled with Jesus. They ate with him. They saw him teaching and healing. They heard him proclaim the Good News of God. They learned from him and were even corrected by him. They even saw him cry, and now they shared the Passover supper with him, the last meal of his life. So fellowship means an honest, open relationship among a close group of friends who care about each other and aid one another in their times of need. The other important part of fellowship is that these small groups are best formed with a church as their foundation.

Level I

Who are your best friends?
What about yourself can you share with them? What can't you?

Level II

If you don't have a close group of friends, what is holding you back?

Is there a small group or youth group at church you can join? If not, why?

How can your being an active participant in fellowship with believers make you more like Jesus?

Maundy Thursday Activity

Share dinner together and attend a Maundy Thursday, Stripping of the Altar service at a church. It is a most powerful and solemn event.

DAY THIRTY-NINE: GOOD FRIDAY

Completion

"It is finished."

(John 19:30 NRSV)

Tetelestai, which is Greek for "it is finished," has several layers of meaning. Looking at each one of them gives a fuller meaning of what Jesus said in his last words. First, it means to complete something or bring to an end. Also, it means to obediently fulfill a rule. Additionally, it means to make a required payment, like taxes or tolls. Finally, it means a period of time is up. So Jesus' last words meant he had completed his task on earth and had obediently followed God's instructions for him. Also, our sins, which keep us away from God, are a debt that needs to be paid, like a toll, and on the cross Jesus paid them for us. Thus, Jesus brought us back to God's family. The truth is that Jesus' last words mean all of that and more. Jesus on the cross said, "It is finished." Though his work on earth was done, really he had only just begun. He lives on and on. His Spirit lives with us, and the Spirit draws us to God.

Level I

Name something good you have completed recently.
How do you feel when you finish something?

Level II

What does Jesus' death on the cross mean to you?
How can you receive his Spirit daily in your life on Earth?

Good Friday Activity

Read one or more of the four gospel accounts of the Jesus death:
Matthew 26:47–28:66
Mark 14:43–15:47
Luke 22:47–23:56
John 18–19

DAY FORTY: HOLY SATURDAY

Rest

> On the Sabbath they rested according to the commandment.
>
> (Luke 24:56b NRSV)

On Friday evening, Joseph of Arimathea, Nicodemus, and the women were at the tomb. The men prepared Jesus' body for burial while the women watched. Then they rolled a large stone in front of the tomb, sealing it shut. They went home and on Saturday they observed the Sabbath. The Torah commands Jews to rest on the Sabbath, which means they are to stay home, not work, and be with their families. So they did. However, it must have been very difficult for them. I doubt they got any rest at all. No, they probably tossed and turned all night long. They tried to eat but couldn't. They tried to sit still, but instead paced. They tried to pray, but no words formed on their lips. They could only cry. They tried to believe, but they couldn't. They thought, *Jesus was really dead. How could it be? What went wrong? How did things get so out of control so quickly? Why did this happen? Why did Jesus die?* These thoughts swirled in their heads. They hoped it was all just a dream. We know the end. We know that on Sunday they ran to the tomb and found it empty, and angels appeared and told them the impossible, the improbable, the incredible. They learned that Jesus was not there. He had risen!

Level I

The Easter egg is a symbol of new life and immortality. How does it remind us of Jesus?

Level II

What does the resurrection mean to you? How has it impacted your life?

How are you learning to have friendship with Jesus each day?

Holy Saturday Activity

Make Easter eggs together. Name some similarities between an Easter egg hunt and the women coming to the tomb on Easter morning.

Put unlit candles all over your house (or the electric type). Wait until Sunday morning to light them all. Then welcome Jesus, the Light of the World into your home and the world!

Endnotes

1. Gardner, Harold, *Multiple Intelligences, New Horizons* (New York: Basic Books, 2006) p. 3
2. Ibid., pp. 5-6.
3. David L. Kirp, "After the Bell Curve," *The New York Times*, July 23, 2006. 2006-10-08. http://www.nytimes.com.
4. Lennick, Doug and Fred Keil, *Moral Intelligence: Enhancing Business Performance and Leadership Success*, (Upper Saddle River, N.J.: Wharton School Publishing, 2005) p. 7.
5. Loehr, Jim and Tony Schwartz, *The Power of Full Engagement: Managing Energy, Not Time, Is the Key to High Performance and Personal Renewal* (New York: The Free Press, 2003) p. 3.

Chapter One
6. Ibid., p. 3.
7. Ibid., p. 5.
8. Ibid., p. 110.
9. Ibid.
10. Ibid.

11. Ibid., p. 201.
12. Ibid., p. 11.
13. Ibid., p. 201.

Chapter Two

14. Wallace, James A., *Preaching to the Hungers of the Heart, The Homily on the Feasts and within the Rites* (Collegeville, Minnesota: The Liturgical Press, 1983) pp. 124-134.
15. Cross, F.L. and E.A. Livingstone eds., *The Oxford Dictionary of the Christian Church*, 3rd ed. (New York: Oxford University Press, 1997) pp. 1444-45.
16. Scott, Lesbia, *I Sing a Song of the Saints of God.* The Church Hymnal Corporation, *The Hymnal 1982, according to the use of The Episcopal Church.* (New York: The Church Hymnal Corporation, 1985) p. 293.
17. Ibid.
18. Ibid.
19. McClurkin, Donnie. "We Fall Down." Live in London And More... . Rec. 22 Aug. 2000. Verity, 2000.
20. Sunderland, Margot, *The Science of Parenting: How Today's Brain Research Can Help You Raise Happy, Emotionally Balanced Children* (New York: DK Publishing Inc., 2006) p. 151.
21. Nolte, Dorothy Law and Rachel Harris, *Children Learn What They Live: Parenting to Inspire Values* (New York: Workman Publishing Company 1999) p. 174.
22. Ibid.
23. Ibid., p. 3.
24. Sears, William and Martha Sears, *The Discipline Book: Everything You Need to Know to Have a Better-Behaved Child* (Boston: Little Brown & Company, 1995) p. 120.
25. Ibid.
26. Ibid., p. 173.

27. Ibid.
28. Tolson, Charles and Harold Koenig, *The Healing Power of Prayer: The Surprising Connection Between Prayer and Your Health* (Grand Rapids, Michigan: Baker Books, 2003) p. 108.

Chapter Three

29. Hagner, Donald A., *Matthew 1-13*, vol. 33a of *World Biblical Commentary,* gen. ed. Bruce M. Metzger (Dallas, Texas: Word Books, 1993) p. 82.
30. Ibid., p. 83.
31. Brown, Raymond E., *An Introduction to the New Testament* (New York: Doubleday, 1997) p. 178.
32. Ibid.
33. Ibid.
34. Schneiders, Sandra, *The Revelatory Text: Interpreting the New Testament as Sacred Scripture* (Collegeville, Minnesota: The Liturgical Press, 1999) p. 28.
35. Ibid., p. 39.

Chapter Four

36. Voltaire, *The Works of Voltaire. A Contemporary Version.* A Critique and Biography by John Morley, notes by Tobias Smollett, trans. William F. Fleming (New York: E.R. DuMont, 1901). In 21 vols. Vol. 6. Chapter: *PRAYER (PUBLIC), THANKSGIVING, ETC.* Accessed from http://oll.libertyfund.org/title/355/62882 on 2007-12-03
37. Kushner, Harold S., *The Lord Is My Shepherd: Healing Wisdom of the Twenty-Third Psalm* (New York: Alfred A. Knopf, 2003) p. 5.
38. Ibid., pp. 6-7.
39. Loehr and Schwartz, p. 166.
40. Ibid.

41. Ibid.
42. Ibid., p. 167.
43. Peck, Scott M., *The Road Less Traveled, 25th Anniversary Edition: A New Psychology of Love, Traditional Values and Spiritual Growth* (New York: Touchstone, 2003) p. 3.
44. Koenig, Harold G., *The Healing Power of Faith: How Belief and Prayer Can Help You Triumph Over Disease* (New York: Touchstone, 1999) p. 24.
45. Ibid.
46. Ibid.
47. The Church Hymnal Corporation, *The Book of Common Prayer, and Administration of the Sacraments and Other Rites and Ceremonies of the Church According to the use of the Episcopal Church* (New York: The Church Hymnal Corporation, 1979) p. 364.
48. St. Francis of Assisi, *"Prayer of St. Francis"*, *Wikipedia*. August 14, 2007. http://en.wikipedia.org/wiki/Prayer_of_Saint_Francis.
49. The Church Hymnal Corporation, *The Book of Common Prayer*. p. 134.
50. Vardey, Lucinda, comp. *Mother Teresa, A Simple Path* (New York: Ballantine Books, 1995) p. 13.
51. Ibid., p. 14.
52. *Billy Graham: Peace with God; The Secret of Happiness; Answer's to Life's Problems: His Greatest Works* (New York: Inspiration Press, 1995) p. 130.
53. Nouwen, Henri J.M., *Here and Now: Living in the Spirit* (New York: Crossroad Publishing Company, 2000) p. 95.
54. Ibid.
55. Nouwen, Henri J.M., *Making All Things New: an Invitation to the Spiritual Life* (San Francisco: Harper San Francisco, 1981) p. 82.
56. Ibid., p. 82-83.

57. Ibid., p. 83.

Chapter Five

58. The Church Hymnal Corporation, The Book of Common Prayer. p. 364-365.
59. Price, Charles P., *Liturgy for Living*, vol. 5 of *The Church's Teaching series* (New York: The Seabury Press, 1979) p. 212,
60. Anglican-Roman Catholic Consultation in the United States, *God's Gift of Unity, A Study Guide for Episcopalians and Roman Catholics, Participant's Book, Draft for Pilot Use in Fall 2004* (New York: Office of Ecumenical and Interfaith Relations, Episcopal Church Center, 2004) p. 88.
61. Mitchell, Leonel L., *Praying Shapes Believing, A Theological Commentary on The Book of Common Prayer* (Harrisburg, Pennsylvania: Morehouse Publishing, 1985) p. 164.
62. The Church Hymnal Corporation, The Book of Common Prayer. p. 102.
63. Mitchell, Leonel L., *Praying Shapes Believing.* p. 181 and Anglican-Roman Catholic Consultation in the United States, *God's Gift of Unity, A Study Guide for Episcopalians and Roman Catholics, Participant's Book, Draft for Pilot Use in Fall 2004.* p.77, 81, 85–88.
64. Ibid.
65. Anglican-Roman Catholic Consultation in the United States, *God's Gift of Unity, A Study Guide for Episcopalians and Roman Catholics, Participant's Book, Draft for Pilot Use in Fall 2004.* p.77.
66. Price, Charles P., p. 210.
67. C.S. Lewis quoted in *Brainyquote*, 2007-12-10. http://www.brainyquote.com/quotes/authors/c/c_s_lewis.html.
68. Smith, Christian with Melinda Denton Lundquist, *Soul Searching: the Religious and Spiritual Lives of American*

Teenagers (New York: Oxford University Press, 2005) p. 56.

69. Frances Vaughan, "What Is Spiritual Intelligence?" *Journal of Humanistic Psychology* 42, (2002): 2, 16-33.

70. Smith, Christian, p. 218-233

71. Ibid.

72. Loehr and Schwartz, p. 110.

73. Ibid., p. 131.

74. *Friberg's Analytical Lexicon of the Greek New Testament*, Complete 2000 edition, *BibleWorks, Program and Databases* CD, version 5.0, rev. 2 (Norfolk, Virginia: BibleWorks, LLC, 2002)

75. Wile, Mary Lee, *I Will, With God's Help, Episcopal Confirmation for Youth and Adults, Leader's Guide* (Denver, Colorado: Living the Good News, 2000) p. 54. Additional information for this activity was drawn from Group Magazine various issues, published by Group Publishing Inc., Loveland, Colorado.

76. Warren, Richard, *The Purpose Driven Life, What on Earth am I Here for?* (Grand Rapids, Michigan: Zondervan, 2002) p. 138.

LaVergne, TN USA
14 August 2009
154940LV00001B/22/P